The Wards

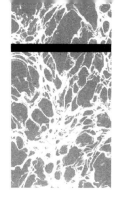

The Wards:
An Introduction to Clinical Clerkships

Paul L. Fine, M.D.
Department of Internal Medicine
University of Michigan Medical School
Ann Arbor

Little, Brown and Company
Boston/New York/Toronto/London

Library of Congress Cataloging-in-Publication Data

Fine, Paul L.
    The wards : an introduction to clinical clerkships / Paul L. Fine.
       p. cm.
    Includes index.
    ISBN 0-316-28322-3
    1. Internal medicine. I. Title
    [DNLM: 1. Clinical Clerkship--handbooks. W 39 F495w 1994]
RC46.F54 1994
610.69'52--dc20
DNLM/DLC
for Library of Congress   94-11844
                                          CIP

Second   Printing

Printed in the United States of America

SEM

Editorial: Evan R. Schnittman
Copyeditor: Elizabeth Willingham
Indexer: Paul L. Fine
Designer: Michael A. Granger
Composition and Production: Silverchair Science + Communications
Cover Designer: Michael A. Granger

To my parents, Marilynn and Burril Fine,
for acts and attributes too numerous to mention

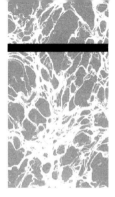

Contents

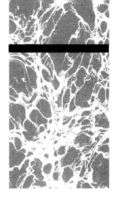

Preface

During the past two years, I have instructed many students who were returning to clinical medicine after spending several years performing doctoral research. From the beginning, I was struck by how difficult it was for these articulate and intelligent students to present cases. Although the method was anything but intuitive, they had received no formal instruction on the proper format and techniques for oral presentations beforehand. With the hope of making the process easier to understand, I wrote an essay to explain the "rules" of oral presentation to these students. Gradually, I added chapters on other facets of the clinical years, often at the suggestion of students and colleagues, until the book lurched into its present form. As I explain in the introductory chapter, my fundamental goal was to ease the traditionally stressful transition between classroom lectures and clinical instruction. An author with such a goal must necessarily address all the issues that concern those who are making the transition. For this reason, I am eager to receive comments and criticisms from readers, particularly their suggestions as to which additional topics merit inclusion in future editions.

As readers will discover from the text, I do believe that word choice has important, sometimes subtle implications. Although I attempted to limit the use of gender-specific pronouns, when it was necessary, I decided arbitrarily to use masculine pronouns when referring to patients (except those with obstetric conditions). Since patients and students are so frequently discussed together, I chose to use feminine pronouns for students for the sake of clarity. In the section on obstetrics, the pronoun roles are reversed. I trust that readers will recognize that no political statement was intended.

P.L.F.

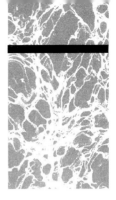

Acknowledgments

I would like to acknowledge (in alphabetical order) the many individuals who have been instrumental in bringing about the successful completion of this project:

Paul J. Davis, a good friend, supplied me with computer software and continual support.

Niraj Desai, a good friend and medical school classmate, critically reviewed the manuscript and offered many valuable suggestions.

Burril Fine, my father, carefully examined two drafts and was responsible for substantial improvements.

David Fine, my brother, provided valuable advice on publication.

Karen Fine, my wife, shared me with the computer for many months and provided encouragement whenever it was needed.

Greg Prokopowicz, a senior medical student at the University of Michigan, read through a final draft and offered many helpful comments.

Eric Ridings, a medical school classmate and friend, read two drafts and made an extraordinary number of valuable suggestions.

Evan R. Schnittman, my editor at Little, Brown and Company, brought enthusiasm and a much-appreciated sense of humor to the project.

Doug Schram, a former colleague in the University of Michigan Internal Medicine Residency Program, graciously allowed me to use his list of acronyms and abbreviations as the foundation for my own.

Elizabeth Willingham, my copyeditor at Silverchair Science + Communications, brought fresh eyes to the manuscript and helped me control my tendency toward ornate prose and verbosity.

James Woolliscroft, who has made great contributions to under-graduate medical education, read an original draft and offered a number of excellent ideas.

Tadataka Yamada, the chairman of the Department of Internal Medicine at the University of Michigan Medical School, was very enthusiastic about bringing the manuscript to publication.

The Wards

Introduction

Rationale and Objectives

Most students identify the clinical years as the highlight of their education. Nevertheless, regardless of the gratification that is eventually attained, the *transition* from the medical school classroom to the hospital ward is difficult for almost every student. Even those who view the lectures and examinations as exasperating obstacles en route to the Promised Land of patient care often find themselves nostalgic for "the good old days" once they reach the hospital. Although there are many reasons for this anxiety, the most significant is the overwhelming uncertainty that seems inextricably linked to their new responsibilities. After all, by the time they have reached the hospital wards, medical students have successfully completed almost 20 years of school and have truly mastered the traditional cycle of lecture, reading, and examination. It is reasonable for them to be apprehensive when this comfortable routine is abruptly interrupted by a mandatory relocation to a new niche and the corresponding necessity to evolve or face extinction. Indeed, Hamlet might have been speaking on behalf of many medical students when he observed that we would "rather bear those ills we have than fly to others that we know not of." Numerous medical schools are now restructuring their curricula to provide an early

1

introduction to the clinical arts; nevertheless, most students will continue to be anxious once they assume clinical responsibilities full-time.

Much of this apprehension is inherent in the transition, for three very understandable reasons:

1. The stakes are higher in the clinical setting. A serious mistake there can cause much more damage than an error on a biochemistry test can.
2. Hospital performance is much more public than performance on a written examination. Students are often concerned about embarrassing themselves in front of their colleagues and superiors.
3. The skills required for effective clinical work are different from those necessary to do well on examinations. Students often lack confidence that they will be sufficiently competent in these new skills.

Although it is experience that will most help students overcome the awkwardness and apprehension, considerable anxiety could be eliminated if they were better informed in advance of the clinical role they are expected to play. This book seeks to facilitate the transition from the classroom to the bedside so that students can spend more time learning medicine and less time trying to comprehend their new ward role.

Two Important Caveats

1. *This book is not intended to serve as a primer of clinical medicine.* The reader will encounter no reviews of procedural techniques, outlines of differential diagnoses, lists of commonly prescribed medications, or other clinical instruction. This information has been omitted for two reasons. First, by making the book lengthy and unwieldy, it would detract from the primary mission of orienting medical students to the broad, rather than the specific, concepts they will need to succeed in their clinical rotations. Second, because there are numerous pocket references that contain this clinical information in compact form, another compilation would surely be superfluous. These pocket books are discussed in Chapter 3 and are highly recommended to the novice clinical clerk.

2. *The approach in this book necessarily reflects my personal views.*

Unlike much of the clinical medicine students will learn during their clerkships, the subject matter in this book is not rooted in unbiased scientific observation. On the wards, there are many ways to do things, no one more objectively "right" than all the others. The considerable variation among medical schools, rotations, and attending physicians makes it impossible to offer descriptions or recommendations that are universally applicable. As much as possible, issues have been discussed in terms that transcend any one rotation or medical school. Nevertheless, because attendings and residents have their own styles and preferences, students will have to adapt to local circumstances and customs.

Overview of Clinical Clerkships

As mentioned above, many American medical schools are actively investigating ways to change their curricula so that their students have earlier and broader experiences in clinical medicine. Nevertheless, the heart of these clinical activities continues to be a student's rotations among various services within the hospital, and this book focuses primarily on the hospital setting. A *service* is a collection of physicians within a certain discipline and their hospitalized patients. Medical students typically spend one or two months working with a particular service, such as neurology, and then relocate to another service, such as surgery, for a similar period of time. The exact order in which they proceed from rotation to rotation will vary, but ultimately each will complete a standard set of core clerkships in addition to any elective clerkships.

Because of the increasing importance of outpatient medical care, more students are getting the opportunity to participate in outpatient clinics during medical school. Although outpatient medical care differs in many ways from the care of hospitalized patients, most of the topics discussed in this book, such as self-education, patient presentations, medical record keeping, and professional standards, are equally important in the outpatient context (see Chapter 11).

A Glossary for the Uninitiated

Authors usually bury glossaries at the end of their books (often in an appendix, which medical students are apt to perceive as a vestigial chapter). Therefore, readers most in need may not discover them until it is too late. So that such readers will know at once of its existence, this book's glossary is provided below. (Although some of these terms are also defined elsewhere in the text, they are included here for the sake of completeness.) This list complements the collection of acronyms and abbreviations provided in the appendix. Those who already are familiar with these definitions may feel free to proceed, via saltatory conduction, to the next chapter. Others may wish to review the terminology now as an introduction to some of the clinical vernacular they will encounter in this book and on the wards.

admit   (1) to arrange for a patient's hospitalization, or (2) to assume care for a newly hospitalized patient. *I plan to admit Mr. Simon tomorrow to the psychiatry service.*

advance directive   a legal document indicating a patient's wishes regarding future medical intervention. *Mr. Kevorkian's advance directive is on the chart.*

ambulatory   see *outpatient.*

arrest   see *code.*

attending   short for "attending physician," the doctor ultimately responsible for a patient's care, whether in the inpatient or outpatient setting. *Who will be serving as Mr. Maxwell's attending—Dr. Horn or Dr. DeGeorgia?*

call   responsibility for admitting new patients to the hospital or evaluating new problems in patients already hospitalized. The term usually refers to nighttime responsibilities. *I was on call last night, so I have only three calls left on this rotation.*

case   (1) a patient's medical history and health problems, or (2) an occurrence of a particular condition. *Derek, I would like your opinion of* *this very interesting case. Tell me if you think Mr. Bun's blue ears indicate cyanosis.*

census   (1) the number of patients in a hospital or on a given ward or service. (2) a listing of these patients. *"We admitted 11 patients today," bragged Freda, "and Mr. Yoshioka brought our census up to 30."*

chart   a patient's medical record. The term may be used for either the main hospital record (containing progress notes, orders, etc.) or a separate document, often referred to as the "bedside chart," on which nurses may record vital signs, fluid intake and output, weights, etc. Some hospitals have implemented electronic charts on their computer systems. *Nurse Pfund, have you seen Mr. Hoffa's chart?*

clinic   a place where nonhospitalized patients undergo medical evaluation. *David, please make Mr. de Bergerac an appointment in the plastic surgery clinic.*

code   (1) a cardiac arrest and its attendant frenzy of therapeutic activity. (2) to suffer a cardiac arrest. *Don't be upset that I didn't answer your page, Jan. I was at a code.*

code status   a patient's status or wishes with regard to the use of cardiopulmonary resuscitation measures. *We had better address code status with Mr. Methuselah.*

complain   to mention a symptom when interviewed. There is no negative connotation associated with the medical use of this term. *Mrs. Murray complains of abdominal pain and vomiting.*

compliance   a patient's tendency to follow the recommendations of physicians. *Mr. Van Winkle has had poor compliance with his medications. He has not taken any of them for the past several decades.*

consultation   also "consult," an informed opinion about a patient's care from someone with specific expertise in the area under consideration. *Eleanor obtained a consultation for Mr.Van Gogh from the ear surgeon.*

contraindication   a reason not to use a particular form of therapy. An "absolute contraindication" is a feature of the case that automatically excludes the possibility of safely using the therapy, whereas a "relative contraindication" is a factor that discourages, but does not forbid, the therapy's use. *Recent brain surgery is an absolute contraindication to the use of thrombolytics in an acute myocardial infarction.*

co-sign   to indicate approval or authorization by adding one's signature to a student's notes, requisitions, or orders. *Dr. Terrell, will you co-sign this order for Mr. Tuschman's blood transfusion?*

crit   a diminutive version of "hematocrit." *You'd better repeat the crit, Niraj, to see if Mr. Tuschman needs another blood transfusion.*

cross-cover   (1) A doctor who assesses problems that develop after a patient's own physicians have gone home. (2) The process of assessing others' patients. *I didn't get much sleep last night because cross-cover was really busy.*

differential diagnosis   a list of the various conditions that might account for a given symptom or sign. *Dr. Winston cocked an eyebrow and rejoined: "Well, Mark, why don't you tell me the differential diagnosis of hypophosphatemia?"*

elective   undertaken without urgency. *Mrs. Rosenbloom is doing much better. We should send her home to recuperate for two weeks and then have her come back for an elective cholecystectomy.*

fellow   a doctor who has completed a residency and is pursuing subspecialty training. *For he's a jolly good cardiology fellow.*

floor   a colloquial term for wards that are not intensive care units. *Dr. Gale says we should transfer Mrs. Von Willebrand to the floor today.*

follow   to participate in the care of a patient. *Gilbert, are you following Mr. Cuthbert?*

follow-up   (1) a patient's future medical appointments or tests. (2) the act of participating in them. *"Abby, have you arranged follow-up for Mr. Katz?" "Yes, he will follow-up with Dr. Doolittle in three weeks."*

H&P   "history and physical," a patient work-up. *I am going to do an H & P on Mrs. Schaberg.*

history   (1) an account of a patient's present and past illnesses. (2) a previous diagnosis. *Mr. Rosenberg has a history of severe degenerative disk disease.*

house officer   also "H.O.," a resident. *Please ask the clerk to page the house officer on call.*

impertinent   not directly related to the problem posed by a patient's chief complaint. *Although it is interesting, Mr. Cyclops' ocular abnormality is impertinent because his chief complaint was indigestion.*

indication   a condition for which a particular therapeutic or pharmacologic intervention is appropriate. *Unexplained fever is an indication for paracentesis in a patient with ascites.*

informant   the individual who supplies a medical history. *Mr. Mitty appeared to be a reliable informant.*

inpatient   (1) occurring during a hospital admission. (2) someone who is hospitalized. *I'm not sure that this hangnail warrants an inpatient evaluation.*

intern   a first-year resident. *The beleaguered intern fell asleep in his mashed potatoes.*

labs   laboratory studies. *Roderick, did you order a serum albumin level among the labs for Mr. Dumpty today?*

line   a colloquial term for an intravenous catheter. *We're going to put a central line in Mrs. Palmer.*

literature   short for "medical research literature." *Dr. Baldoni has asked me to look up the recent literature on coronary artery stents.*

lytes   a diminutive form of "electrolytes," a laboratory test panel consisting of serum sodium, potassium, chloride, and bicarbonate (and in some hospitals, magnesium, calcium, and phosphorus) levels. *Poor Mr. Kringle—admitted for chest pain on December 25. He's on a diuretic, so we had better order some Christmas lytes.*

manage   to direct the care of a given patient or of one of his medical conditions. *Dr. Blitz is managing Mr. Harrison's renal failure.*

meds   a colloquial term for "medications." *Tell Mr.*

Nastelin that he shouldn't take his meds with beer.

note see progress note.

orders statements from a patient's physician that indicate the specific nursing, pharmacologic, and laboratory interventions he or she desires for the patient. *Please be sure to include allopurinol in the admitting orders for Mr. Franklin.*

outpatient (1) occurring outside the hospital setting. (2) someone who is undergoing medical evaluation outside of a hospital. *I think Mr. Minard can be worked up as an outpatient for his incapacitating fear of tigers.*

path short for "pathology results." *Has the path come back on Mrs. Smith's liver biopsy?*

pertinent useful in analyzing a patient's chief complaint. *"My dear Holmes," Dr. Watson said smugly, "the absence of fever is clearly pertinent in this case of unexplained abdominal pain."*

pick up to participate in the care of. *Liz, I'd like you to pick up our new patient, Mrs. Edinger.*

present (1) to tell someone about a case in a formal manner. (2) to come to medical attention. *Dr. Zhivago, let me present this case to you. Mr. Geruce is a previously healthy 30-year-old man who presents with wrist and hand pain after 10 hours of typing at his computer.*

progress note a brief summary of a patient's condition. *Emily, would you write Mrs. Abramson's progress note today?*

resident a doctor in a postgraduate specialty training

program. *Trevor wrapped his arms around Jessica, pressed his lips to her ear, and whispered, "After medical school, my darling, I plan to become a urology resident."*

rotation   a period of time during which a student works with a particular service. *Jennifer enjoyed her neonatology rotation because she got to hold so many babies.*

round   to visit patients in a systematic fashion. *I am going to round on my patients again this afternoon.*

rounds   a congregation of medical personnel for a specific purpose. *Tammi hurried to grand rounds to hear Dr. Strangelove's lecture on movement disorders.*

scut   a very popular colloquial term for the routine tasks required in patient care. *With three blood samples to draw, four x-rays to find, and three sets of staples to remove, I have enough scut to keep me here until midnight.*

service   (1) a collection of physicians within a certain discipline and their hospitalized patients. (2) the group of patients one is caring for. *"Because I have only two patients on my service," Beth chirped merrily, "I may get out in time to go dancing tonight."*

sign   an abnormality of physical examination or laboratory testing detected by a trained observer. *Yes, Eve, Mr. Parker's spider angiomata are a sign of chronic liver disease.*

spike   to develop a fever (colloquial). *Mr. Jones spiked last night.*

stat   immediately. *Gadzooks, Eric, I think you've*

punctured the lung! Call for a chest x-ray stat, and then phone the hospital attorney.

status post having had a particular medical procedure. *Mr. Hart is a 64-year-old man with a history of ischemic cardiac disease, status-post coronary artery bypass surgery, who presented with three hours of continuous chest pain.*

symptom an abnormal sensation or phenomenon noted by a patient. *When Mimi and Violetta presented to the emergency room, their main symptoms were fever, cough, and weight loss.*

teaching hospital a hospital in which patient care is delivered at least in part by supervised residents and medical students. Despite what the phrase suggests, the hospital itself does not do any of the teaching. *I'm sorry about your hand, Captain Hook, but these things sometimes happen in a teaching hospital.*

transfer (1) to shift the care of a patient from one team to another. (2) a patient whose care has been shifted from one team to another. *Now that his pneumonia has been fully treated, Mr. Quasimodo will be transferred to the orthopedics service for back surgery.*

unit "intensive care unit." *Mr. Kent has had a significant exposure to kryptonite. We'd better admit him to the unit.*

ward a hospital unit of approximately 20 to 40 beds often designated for a particular type of patient. *Mrs. Malaprop was admitted to the neurology ward with a stroke.*

work-up (1) the evaluation of a patient with an interview, physical examination, and selected laboratory studies. (2) to evaluate a patient.

(3) the written summary of the evaluation. *"Julia, did you work up Mrs. Berg?" "Yes, Matt, I'll be giving you my work-up to review later this afternoon."*

write-up a written case presentation. *Julia, where is that write-up you promised me?*

Conspicuously absent from this glossary are many slang terms and expressions that students will undoubtedly encounter in their clinical work—"gomer," "gorked," "bad hit," and "dump," for example. These expressions have been excluded because they are disrespectful of patients and foster an "us against them" mentality that subtly encourages students to perceive patients collectively as a dehumanized enemy. There is no doubt that students and residents are sometimes overworked and overwrought. The training system does make demands on them that can seem unreasonable. *But it is not the patients' fault.* The language of the wards should not suggest otherwise.

2

The Hospital Environment

Wildlife television programs often focus on a particular habitat and document the many kinds of organisms that live there and their interrelations. This brief chapter provides a similar analysis of the teaching hospital environment. I have resisted the considerable temptation to assign animal metaphors to each role.

Wards

Hospitals are divided into separate *wards*, units of approximately 20 to 40 beds often designated for patients with particular types of problems. Thus, a hospital might have separate cardiology wards, surgical wards, or neurology wards. Each ward is, to a degree, an independent patient care organization with its own clerical staff and nurses. There are usually two centers of activity, the doctors' conference room and the clerical station where the patients' medical records ("charts") are kept. Adjacent to the charts, one can find a variety of products that help keep paper manufacturers in business: diagnostic study requisitions, progress note sheets, order forms, prescription pads, and so forth. Most wards have a supply room containing suture, needles, catheters, gauze, intravenous fluids, and the other materiel that patient care demands. Hospital computer terminals are usually available on the wards as well.

Ward Clerks

A good ward clerk is essential for the efficient operation of a ward. Clerks are responsible for transmitting orders to the individuals who will implement them. They also answer telephone calls, request patients' prior records from the medical records department, prepare charts for patients at the time of admission, stock them with the necessary forms, and dismantle them when a patient is discharged. In short, ward clerks manage the varied minutiae that are collectively vital to the proper functioning of the ward.

Nurses

Nurses carry out most of the details of the patient care plan, from changing wound dressings to administering medications. Because they spend so much time with patients, they frequently have a finely developed sense for when a patient's condition is about to deteriorate. In addition, they may have vast experience in managing certain special problems such as wound care, chemotherapy-induced nausea, or cardiac arrhythmias. Physicians who make excellent patient care their first priority therefore view nursing colleagues as partners in patient management.

Nursing Hierarchy

There are various levels of training in nursing. The most common, in ascending order of required education, are nurses' aide, licensed practical nurse (LPN), and registered nurse (RN). In some parts of the country, the middle level is occupied by licensed vocational nurses (LVN). Some tasks may be performed only by nurses with a greater amount of training. Thus, although an LPN or nurses' aide might measure a patient's vital signs or assist with a bath, only an RN may be permitted to administer certain medications or to accept orders from the medical team via telephone. Some nurses have advanced training in a specific area, such as chemotherapy or intensive care.

Medical Student–Nurse Relations

Occasionally, when nurses believe they have been treated poorly by attendings or residents but cannot express their anger to the medical staff, they may direct it instead toward an unfortunate medical student who is blameless. The student should try not to take this sort of incident personally. Certainly, the exchange can happen in the reverse direction: A medical student who has been frustrated by patients or physicians may project anger instead toward a nurse. Hospitals can be stressful places because of the stern demands of patient care; those working there must obviously try to get along with one another.

Medical students must remember that nurses are not permitted to accept verbal or written orders from them. They should not feel insulted; nurses are similarly prohibited from accepting orders from architects, novelists, senators, and anyone else without a medical license.

The Medical Hierarchy

There is a hierarchy within the medical ranks, just as there is within the armed forces. Each position has its own set of responsibilities, and physicians in training are gradually promoted from one position to the next.

Attending Physician

An *attending physician* ("attending," for short) is a fully trained and licensed doctor who supervises trainees in a teaching hospital or an outpatient clinic. The attending physician who takes charge of a given hospital case may be the patient's clinic physician ("private attending") or a hospital or medical school staff physician who has been given responsibility for hospitalized patients for a one- or two-month period ("teaching attending"). A teaching attending usually holds educational conferences ("attending rounds") with the ward team (see Chapter 3).

The ward attending is ultimately responsible for every aspect of the patient's care and is therefore given the authority to make all medical decisions. In most instances, however, the attending is involved in the initial decision-making on only the most important issues, such as whether to proceed with surgery, whether to obtain a special diagnostic study, or whether to discharge the patient from the hospital. Lesser decisions, such as which blood tests to order for the next day and how much potassium chloride to administer, are usually made by a fellow or senior resident, subject to the attending's review and approval.

Fellows and Residents

Some services (especially consultation services) have a *fellow*, a physician who has completed residency and entered a subspecialty training program to pursue research and/or further clinical training. *Residents* (also known as *house officers*) have completed medical school and are at various stages in a postgraduate specialty training program in fields such as surgery, pediatrics, or psychiatry. Traditionally, first-year residents are known as *interns*. Senior residents are responsible for supervising, in a more detailed way than the attending, the daily care of the patients on a service. They direct morning rounds and assign the care of patients to junior residents and medical students. They also perform much of the teaching of medical students. The most junior physicians on the service, typically interns, are given the responsibility of implementing the team's plans for patient care. They assess their patients frequently, schedule studies, perform procedures, and write progress notes and orders. In most cases, it is the intern who is informed first about any changes in a patient's condition.

Medical Students

On some services, there will be a *subintern*, a senior medical student who functions as an intern under the close supervision of the team's senior resident (see Chapter 12). The third-year medical students, or *clinical clerks*, work closely with the most junior physicians in implementing the team's plans for patient care. On most medical and pediatric services, students primarily follow the patients they worked up at the time of admission. On some surgical services, they are expected instead to participate with other team members in the care of the entire service. Their daily responsibilities include writing the progress note and orders, presenting the patient at morning rounds, assessing any new problems, obtaining test results, and facilitating care in any other way necessary (see Chapter 9).

Others

Most hospitals employ a number of specialists who are able to provide expert advice and assistance to physicians on certain aspects of patient care. These include other physicians ("consultants"), dietitians, respiratory therapists, pharmacists, physical therapists, social workers, and patient advocates. Such specialists often make substantial contributions to patient management; moreover, they provide a valuable resource for the student who has questions about one of their areas of expertise.

Many hospitals also have phlebotomy and IV teams, personnel who are specially trained in the drawing of blood and/or the placement of intravenous catheters. Such teams greatly facilitate patient care, but overreliance on them may take from medical students vital experience in performing these fundamental procedures. Therefore, students should draw blood and insert IV catheters themselves whenever possible, at least until they become proficient in the techniques. After all, when they become interns, they are likely to be called on whenever the phlebotomy team has been unsuccessful.

3

Education

Reading

Few lectures are given amid the fever and the fret of hospital wards. Therefore, the educational process there is quite different from that with which students have been familiar. Books and medical journals replace lectures as the primary source of information, and it becomes the student's responsibility to choose appropriate reading selections. Although the process of self-education will be important for the rest of their professional lives, many students are initially frustrated by their uncertainty about what to read.

Patient-Directed Reading

Some students choose a textbook of some kind and endeavor to complete it during their time on a given ward service. This technique, which best approximates the style of learning they are accustomed to, can be successful as long as the textbook is written for students and is not overly laden with detail. If time runs short, students can ask residents and attendings which topics are particularly important.

A better overall approach, though, is to allow the reading to be directed by the illnesses of the patients one is caring for. The chief advantage of this method is that it gives the student a story and a face with which to associate the facts about a given condition. Most people find that they retain more of their reading when they can employ a framework of personal experience. There are other advantages as well. Patient-directed reading helps students develop skills that will prove useful when they encounter unfamiliar conditions or problems in the future. It also familiarizes them with the palpable excitement engendered by investigating the literature with the goal of improving a particular patient's chances for diagnosis or successful therapy. *Above all, this approach emphasizes that reading is a supplement to clinical experience, not a surrogate.* One should always learn as much as possible from the clinical activities arising from patient care. Reading may be deferred to a time of clinical quiescence.

If students' reading selections are determined by their patients' problems, they are limited by the number and variety of their cases. It is therefore important that they view each case as an opportunity to read broadly. For example, if a patient is admitted with a diabetic foot ulcer, one should read not only about diabetic foot ulcers, but also about other complications of diabetes, other causes of cutaneous ulcers, and principles of antimicrobial therapy. Similarly, a patient with peptic ulcer disease should prompt an inquiry into the differential diagnosis of abdominal pain and the various studies that can be used to differentiate among the possibilities. In this way, a student can abide by the principle of reading foremost about his or her own cases and simultaneously broaden the scope of the knowledge acquired in the process. Often, students become too narrowly focused and, like residents and attendings, limit their reading to the current controversies in a given field. Although it is rewarding to participate in this sort of state-of-the-art literature review, the latest research generally serves the student less well than review articles and chapters from highly regarded textbooks.

Differential Diagnosis

In each case, no matter how "obvious" the diagnosis, the student should read about the *differential diagnosis* for the major presenting symptoms and signs. The differential diagnosis is a list of various conditions that could account for features of a patient's illness. In the early part of medical school, most students are taught that disease A is associated with manifestations X, Y, and Z and that disease B is associated with manifestations S, T, and X. Patients, however, will complain of manifestation X much more often than they will proclaim that they have disease B. Therefore, students cannot assist these patients until they learn how to reason "backwards" from manifestation X to the diseases in its differential diagnosis, A and B. The development of this ability through discussion and reading should be one of their primary goals. An excellent resource is the weekly "Case Records of the Massachusetts General Hospital" in the *New England Journal of Medicine*, in which a case presentation is followed by an experienced clinician's discussion of differential diagnosis.

Reference Books

There are two basic classes of clinical medical books. First, there are books dedicated to a single specialty, such as a textbook of surgery or a review of pediatrics. The comprehensive texts in each field are often extraordinarily long and expensive, so most students buy a less weighty paperback book instead and refer to the tomes only when necessary. Many publishers now offer series of paperback books that cover the important topics in different specialties. These include the "For the House Officer" books, the Appleton & Lange handbooks, the NMS series, and the Little, Brown spiral manuals. For any given rotation, it is best to seek advice about which book to use from a resident or a student who has (successfully) completed the rotation.

Second, there are books that contain useful information not specific to any one specialty or rotation. This category includes basic primers on interviewing and physical diagnosis, electrocardiogram interpretation, and radiography, as well as those replete with practical information such as medication indications and dosages, procedural techniques, formulae, and lists of differential diagnoses for common symptoms. Among the basic primers, many students prefer the *A Guide to Physical Examination and History Taking* by Barbara Bates, *Rapid Interpretation of EKG's* by Dale Dubin, and *Fundamentals of Radiology* by Lucy Squire and Robert Novelline. For books of the "clinical-data-at-one's-fingertips" variety, most students use Jay Sanford's *Guide to Antimicrobial Therapy* and either *Clinician's Pocket Reference* ("the scut monkey's handbook," edited by Leonard Gomella), the *Manual of Medical Therapeutics* ("the Washington Manual," by the Washington University Department of Medicine), or *A Practical Guide to the Care of the Medical Patient* (no nickname, edited by Fred Ferri). Each of the last three is an excellent reference and will greatly assist the student who keeps a copy (alongside this book) in his or her lab coat pocket and becomes intimately familiar with it. One must avoid the tendency to buy several such books as a salve for insecurity, because invariably one of two bad outcomes occurs. Either some of the books are purchased but never used (a waste of money), or each one is used occasionally and a student never gains the advantage of becoming thoroughly familiar with any of them (a waste of time).

Finding Time to Read

Students are expected to give their clinical responsibilities highest priority. In many cases, these responsibilities leave so little time for reading that students become frustrated. During the day, *it may be futile to wait for an uninterrupted stretch of one or two hours to use for reading*. Instead, students should take advantage of the numerous 10- or 15-minute intervals that occur in the average day to "read on the run." These periods, when supplemented by some dedicated time outside the hospital, should be sufficient for them to read about their patients' problems in a timely manner.

Attending Rounds

Attending rounds are sessions in which the team meets with the supervising, or "attending," physician to accomplish two goals: patient care and team education. The discussion is usually focused on patients who have recently been admitted to the service, and medical students are responsible for presenting the cases (see Chapters 6 and 7). The format chosen for these rounds varies among attendings, but most instruct their teams using the Socratic method of extended questioning. Therefore, a medical student can expect that his or her answers will lead inexorably to further questions. Although students must prepare themselves for this exercise through reading and discussion, they should understand that nobody expects them to answer every question correctly. In fact, an attending often asks certain difficult questions just to introduce the next topic of instruction.

Without exception, questions must be answered truthfully. If a student does not know a laboratory result, she should say so and resist the temptation to say "it was normal." Similarly, if asked whether a certain physical finding was present, a student who failed to look for it must admit that she does not know. There is no shame in failing to recognize the importance of a laboratory result or a physical finding; this is one way that students learn from their attendings. There is an abundance of shame in deception, however. Such an act brings negative implications about one's character and integrity and, more important, can harm a patient if the attending physician makes decisions based on the inaccurate information provided.

Learning from Patients

As discussed in Chapter 5, students generally find that they have limited time with newly admitted patients. Therefore, they must often direct their initial interviews toward areas that seem immediately relevant. In later discussions, however, they should take the opportunity to expand the scope of their questions into other topics, including those that contribute more to student education than to patient management. For example, if a patient with a past history of glomerulonephritis is admitted with angina, the initial questioning should of course be focused on the cardiac complaints. The characterization of the symptoms that originally led to the diagnosis of glomerulonephritis is certainly unlikely to be helpful in the management of the chest pain. Nevertheless, the student who pursues this characterization in a follow-up discussion with the patient will gain a valuable lesson in the natural history of glomerulonephritis. Similarly, when a cancer patient is admitted for his seventh cycle of "routine" chemotherapy, a student can make the case more educational by asking the patient what caused doctors to suspect cancer in the first place.

Others' Patients
Students can also learn from patients they are not following themselves. The easiest way to do this is to pay attention when these patients are discussed during rounds. When unfamiliar concepts are mentioned, one should make a note of the subjects and investigate them at the next opportunity; a useful rule to follow is "if you

don't understand something, ask someone or look it up within 24 hours." Similarly, if a student hears that a patient has an unusual or interesting physical finding, she should introduce herself to the patient and ask for permission to elicit the finding.

When on call, a student can learn a great deal by accompanying interns or residents when they are called urgently to evaluate a problem. These situations offer a "purer" exercise of diagnostic abilities than do many admitting evaluations, because one is not informed of another physician's opinion before starting the work-up. Instead, one is called to see an unfamiliar patient because of some acute change in his status and must quickly perform a directed interview and physical examination and decide on a course of action. By participating in this process, a student can learn how urgent evaluations are done and see how doctors approach some common medical problems.

Questions

Resident and attending physicians are useful sources of information and explanations; the majority are eager to answer questions from students at any time. Most medical students ask questions too infrequently, either because they are embarrassed or because they do not wish to risk appearing ignorant to those who will grade their performances. This concern is counterproductive, however, because residents and attendings realize that all students have topics with which they are unfamiliar. A student who does not ask questions is usually thought to be uninterested or intimidated, whereas the inquisitive student is respected for having a desire to learn.

When a resident or attending is demonstrating an abnormality such as a patient's enlarged spleen or a pericardial rub, it is important that a student be honest about whether she too appreciates it. If the finding remains obscure, she should ask to be shown again. Her evaluators are unlikely to write: "She took excellent care of her patients and read thoroughly about their conditions. She was well liked by team members and worked harmoniously with all hospital personnel. Nevertheless, she failed to perceive Mr. Keats' enlarged spleen on palpation and so it is my recommendation that she repeat the entire clerkship."

Conferences

Most clinical services provide educational conferences or lectures for their residents and medical students, often during the noon lunch hour. Obviously, students benefit from attending these conferences whenever possible. But what if going to the conference would necessitate missing an important part of a patient's assessment and management? Because patient care provides the most important clinical lessons and is always given highest priority, the following is a useful rule: Those patient care issues that must be attended to immediately should take precedence over the conference. However, if the clinical responsibilities can safely wait for an hour or so, one should always attend the lecture. Although it may be difficult, a student should resist the temptation to miss a conference "just this once" because of fatigue and a desire to complete the day's work quickly and leave the hospital earlier. Once one begins to think this way, it will be easy to find equally valid reasons to skip almost every conference.

Learning How to Learn

The process of self-education and the ability to generate differential diagnoses are among the most important things students learn as clinical clerks. Even if they never again use the knowledge acquired in the process, they will have mastered the techniques of inquiry necessary for future clinical endeavors.

4

The Interview and Physical Examination

There are many excellent books devoted to interviewing and physical examination (*The Clinical Approach to the Patient*, by Morgan and Engel, is particularly valuable); this chapter is not intended to supplant them. Its description of these fundamental medical skills will focus more on process than on content, especially the modifications that must often be made within the setting of the teaching hospital. Students who wish to keep with them a reminder of the basic components of the history and physical examination will find summaries on the detachable card at the end of the book.

The Interview

In many respects, interviewing is the core of the art of medicine. The physician continually chooses between asking and listening, directing and following. Above all, the student should remember that it is a dynamic process that must be continuously modified based on the information received. The interviewer is actually carrying on two distinct conversations simultaneously. One conversation is with himself, in which he asks and answers questions such as "What else do I need to know about this symptom?" and "What sorts of conditions can cause this symptom and which questions will help me differentiate among them?" The second conversation, of course, is the overt one with the patient that influences, and is itself influenced by, its tacit counterpart.

The tone of the interview has great importance. A therapeutic relationship between doctor and patient begins with an interview that is conducted with sympathy, gentle authority, and a willingness to let the conversation drift now and again to topics that are not overtly medical. The physician must avoid the tendency to become a question-asking automaton in the pursuit of efficiency. Such a style is better suited to a pollster than to a physician. Similarly, it is wise to avoid taking notes excessively while interviewing, especially during the discussion of the history of the present illness. This practice, which tends to disrupt continuity, avert eye contact, and inhibit disclosure, may thwart the more humane elements of the interaction. One should make notes sparingly and record other information *after* the interview is completed.

Directed Interview

Because time and patients' tolerance are limited, especially in the setting of acute illness, most interviews must be *directed* to some extent; that is, they must focus on the issues that appear to be most relevant and ignore some other areas. This approach may frustrate the more compulsive students, who would prefer to ask as many different questions as possible and therefore avoid the responsibility of choosing which areas are relevant and which are not. With time, they will become more comfortable with this inevitable limitation; through reading and discussion, they will learn what is important. At the start of their careers, however, they will often need to return to a patient's room for further questioning after their research has uncovered additional areas of relevance.

In a directed interview, the "follow-up question" assumes a particularly important role. For example, if a patient confirms that he sleeps on two pillows each night, one cannot conclude that he has orthopnea and proceed to the next question. Instead, the reason for the consistent use of two pillows must be explored. Is it truly a sense of suffocation or dyspnea? Is it gastroesophageal reflux symptoms that occur when he is lying flat? Is it merely comfort or habit? A follow-up question such as "What happens when you try to sleep *without* your pillows?" will allow the interviewer to reach whatever conclusion is warranted.

Prior Records

A patient's prior medical records, which are sometimes referred to as the "old chart," can be a very useful supplement to the information obtained in the interview. In most cases, however, a neophyte clinical clerk should avoid reading them before the interview, thereby vanquishing the temptation to obtain the past medical history through the succinct impressions of other medical professionals instead of the meandering, incomplete, and medically unsophisticated recollections provided by some patients. Students who make a good-faith effort to obtain information on their own before consulting prior records will gain valuable experience in interviewing and be better prepared for the many complicated cases in which prior records are unavailable. Once they have reviewed an old chart, students will often want to return to a patient's room to ask additional questions.

Despite this general rule, there are certain situations in which an examination of prior records may reasonably replace a portion of the interview: (1) when a frustrated patient protests a student's attempts to untangle a complicated past medical history ("Why don't you look it up? It's all there in my records."); and (2) when an experienced senior student acting as a subintern must conduct the interview and physical examination as quickly and efficiently as possible.

Sequence of Topics

There is no law mandating that all interviews proceed from chief complaint to history of present illness to past medical history, and so forth. The packaging of historical data into these discrete, ordered sections is a somewhat arbitrary process undertaken principally for oral and written presentations. During the interview itself, one will frequently find that it is easier to discuss a topic when it arises, regardless of its eventual location in the presentation, because interviews with too much imposed structure tend to be discontinuous and awkward. An interviewer who is following the usual sequence of topics may of course delete questions that have been answered earlier in the interview during such "topical tangents."

Breaking the Ice

A successful doctor-patient relationship depends on a patient's levels of trust and comfort. Therefore, most patients and physicians prefer to spend a little time chatting before conducting the more formal parts of the interview. Though the topic of this exchange is less important than its tone, the experience may still prove enlightening to a clinician who is trying to understand the patient as well as the illness.

Chief Complaint

The chief complaint is usually the answer to a question such as "What brings you here today?" or "How may I help you?" Unfortunately, identifying a patient's chief complaint is not always straightforward. There are two particular circumstances in which students may find it unexpectedly difficult to make this designation:

1. They may discover that the chief complaint is unrelated to the reason for hospitalization. For example, a patient may complain primarily of abdominal pain and nausea despite the fact that she had been admitted to the hospital for treatment of osteomyelitis. Another may be admitted for an elective cholecystectomy without any symptoms at all. The student should keep in mind the distinction between the chief complaint and the reason for hospitalization.

2. A patient may have multiple complaints and be unable to assign highest priority to any of them at the inception of the interview. In such a case, it may become clear as the conversation progresses which symptoms are particularly important to him. Rarely, if the history remains murky, the clinician may have to wait until physical examination and laboratory data are available to designate a chief complaint. For example, consider a patient who responds affirmatively to virtually every question in the review of systems. It may be impossible to discern which complaints are most important, even at the conclusion of the interview. However, if subsequent physical and laboratory examinations suggest a diagnosis of pyelonephritis, the student may wish to extract fever, dysuria, and flank pain from the dozens of other symptoms to serve as the ele-

ments of the chief complaint. In this situation, because the choice of a chief complaint reflects the student's assessment of other data, there is always the risk that an incorrect assessment will prompt an inappropriate selection of a chief complaint. A student shouldn't worry too much about this risk; occasional errors in reasoning are to be expected as part of clinical training.

History of Present Illness

The history of present illness (HPI) is the most important part of the history, yet it is easy for students to "lose control" of the interview at this stage. The following are recommendations on how to elicit the HPI effectively.

1. *Observe the patient and listen carefully;* avoid the tendency to try to write everything down as it is being said. Subtleties of expression or inflection may be as informative as the words themselves.

2. As much as possible, allow the patient to tell the story without interruption. After listening for a few minutes, supplement the information by asking follow-up questions. Usually, one begins with open-ended queries ("Tell me more about the chest discomfort") and then refines the history with more specific questions ("Was the chest discomfort accompanied by nausea?").

3. Remember to avoid using medical terms the patient is unlikely to know ("Have you had any tinnitus along with your phonophobia, Mrs. Morrison?").

4. Help the patient be as specific as possible about when, and in what order, events occurred. However, try not to be influenced by a patient's suppositions regarding causality, because a patient will often inappropriately transform a temporal association into a causal one ("I took two of those red pills, Doctor, and they made me short-winded").

5. Ask patients to characterize their symptoms in as much detail as they can. If a patient mentions abdominal pain, be sure eventually to learn exactly when it started, how long it persisted, where it was located, what it felt like, how severe it was, and what factors palliated or provoked it. If the patient has dyspnea on exertion, discover exactly which activities typically induce it.

6. Ask the important "differential questions" as they arise in your mind, even if they include elements of the past medical history, social history, family history, or review of systems. Differential questions are defined and discussed in Chapter 6.

7. Periodically summarize important topics ("Mr. Janeway, let me see if I have understood you correctly. You first noticed chest discomfort six weeks ago while mowing your lawn . . ."). This practice ensures accuracy and often helps a patient to remember additional important details. It also gives the student some practice prior to an oral presentation of the case.

8. Although the best approach is usually chronological, it may be necessary to forsake it with patients who have numerous, long-standing complaints. In such cases, discuss each issue separately with the patient for the sake of clarity. If a symptom is intermittent, characterize the most recent episode first and ask the patient to compare other episodes to it.

Past Medical History

The clinician generally begins this portion of the interview with a question such as "Other than the things we have just discussed, what medical problems have you had?" Each prior illness or condition is then discussed in turn. Some guidelines may prove useful:

1. In the initial interview, a student should focus primarily on the "big issues": How long ago was an illness diagnosed? How severe has it been? Are there objective tests documenting changes in severity over a period of time? How has it been treated? Has the treatment made a difference, subjectively or objectively? Have there been any complications? Questions (and answers) about the symptoms and diagnostic tests that initially led to diagnosis are edifying but not immediately helpful unless the original diagnosis is in question. For this reason, they are often postponed until later discussions.

2. Once patients have finished describing their past problems, it may be helpful to prompt them further with general ("When were you last hospitalized? Have you ever had surgery?") or specific ("Have you had any problems with your heart or lungs?") questions. Note that the specific questions in this case refer to *diagnosed* conditions or illnesses, not symptoms. Symptoms that have not yet been coupled to a diagnosis are discussed as part of the review of systems.

3. Because patients frequently have trouble outlining their past medical history, a review of their prior records after the interview may be necessary to ensure accuracy and completeness.

Medications and Adverse Reactions to Medications

The inquiry about medications and adverse reactions to medications should be one of the most straightforward in the interview, but it sometimes presents difficulty:

1. Most patients have trouble remembering the names and dosages of several medications. If recent medical records are available, they will fill in any information gaps nicely. Otherwise, it is often useful for an outpatient, or a relative of an inpatient, to bring in medication bottles from home for review. When a patient can remember only some general information ("I'm taking a blood pressure pill" or "I'm on Synthroid but I don't know the size of the pill"), the clinician may try to spark recognition by listing some possibilities or showing the patient the medication photographs published in the *Physicians' Desk Reference* ("the PDR").

2. Medical students are likely to be frustrated by the fact that they know medications by names different from those used by patients ("furosemide" instead of "Lasix," for example). In the first clinical months, students will often need to write down the trade names given by their patients and look up the generic counterparts after the interview is completed.

3. Patients will sometimes fail to mention over-the-counter medications, such as vitamins and cold remedies, unless asked about them explicitly.

4. When a patient mentions a medication allergy, the clinician should always ask about the reaction. Many "allergies" are really nonallergic adverse reactions, such as diarrhea or headache. Sometimes a clinician will want to ask specifically about certain allergies that would necessitate a change in the current management plan, such as a penicillin allergy in a patient who will need antibiotic therapy or a shellfish allergy in a patient who is scheduled to receive intravenous contrast dye.

Family History

The family history is most important in answering two questions: (1) Have any close relatives had similar symptoms or a disease of the organ system that is the suspected culprit? (2) Have any close relatives had common diseases for which there is a significant component of heritability, such as diabetes mellitus or coronary artery disease? Pedigree symbols, which are demonstrated in Chapter 8, are a convenient way to record the family history.

Social History
The social history elucidates a patient's life-style and habits. It supplies the information necessary to convert him from a collection of medical data to an actual person. Elements of the social history will often be covered during the informal conversation that precedes the interview or during asides in the interview itself. If they are not, general inquiries such as "How do you spend your time?" and "Tell me more about yourself" can be useful in initiating the process. Appropriate topics for direct questions include sexual history, marital status, occupation and occupational exposures, exercise, hobbies, diet, and the use of tobacco, alcohol, and other drugs. The sexual history must be approached with care. After an introductory question such as "Do you find your sexual life satisfying?" note-taking should be suspended and one should watch for nonverbal clues that suggest a desire to expand or limit the discussion of this topic. With regard to alcohol consumption, it is important to remember that alcohol's effect on a patient's life can be a more sensitive indicator of a problem than the exact amount consumed. Smoking is usually quantified in pack-years, the product of the number of packs smoked on a typical day and the duration of the patient's cigarette use in years.

Review of Systems
The review of systems is a series of questions regarding symptoms the patient may have had recently ("Have you had difficulty swallowing? Any abdominal pains, vomiting?", etc.). The questions are segregated by organ system and can be asked in rapid succession as long as the answers are negative. If one of the questions draws a positive response, the clinician must interrupt the sequence and characterize the symptom further in the usual ways. It is particularly helpful to know the time course over which a symptom has developed. Did it begin last week and worsen rapidly, or has it been present intermittently since World War II? Though the review of systems is usually performed as the last step in the history, an interviewer will commonly ask many of the questions earlier during discussion of the present illness. There is no need to repeat any questions that have already been answered.

Some clinicians prefer to perform the review of systems as they do the corresponding portions of the physical examination. This approach works well, as long as most of the questions are answered negatively. Too many pauses for the clarification of positive answers will disrupt the continuity of the physical examination.

The Last Question

Before concluding the interview, one should ask "Is there anything we have not discussed that you would like to mention?" This broad invitation gives the patient another opportunity to disclose any information he had previously forgotten or was reluctant to share with the interviewer.

The Physical Examination

The Directed Physical Examination

As with the inpatient interview, the inpatient physical examination must be a compromise between thoroughness and practicality. Novices always benefit from performing as complete an examination as possible; this practice helps them learn what constitutes "normal" and what constitutes "abnormal." Most of the time, however, students must limit the initial examination due to time constraints or patient intolerance. In these cases, they should confer with the intern or resident and at least elicit any abnormal features of the examination that might change rapidly. The rest of the examination can usually be completed later. For example, if a patient is admitted with severe congestive heart failure and needs urgent diuresis, the student should quickly assess jugular venous distention, listen for pulmonary crackles and cardiac gallops, and note the degree of hepatomegaly or peripheral edema so that he or she can observe how these findings change with treatment.

Even when a student has the luxury of performing a truly complete examination, he or she should first use the information learned in the interview to create hypotheses about what will be discovered during any given part of the process. The examination will then be an opportunity to test these hypotheses. By thinking in advance about the implications of various parts of the examination, the student can ensure that the data most important to the case are accurately obtained.

Initial Awkwardness

There is no substitute for experience. During their initial attempts at physical examination, students are likely to have difficulty with the techniques and the interpretation of their findings. Their examinations will be somewhat disjointed and will take a long time to perform. After all, it is one thing to practice a physical examination on a classmate who is a healthy, thin, mobile friend; it is quite another to perform one on a hospitalized patient who is a sick, overweight, relatively immobile stranger. Fortunately, patients are usually very understanding, unless they are feeling particularly tired or uncomfortable, and students should feel free to repeat portions of the examination that they find difficult, as long as their patients are comfortable. To gain confidence and competence, students may also want to practice on colleagues; this will help them memorize the proper sequence of the examination and familiarize themselves with diagnostic equipment such as stethoscopes, ophthalmoscopes, and sphygmomanometers.

General Principles

1. The clinician's thoughtful attention need not be limited to the formal portion of the physical examination. There is much to be learned from watching a patient walk, observing his interactions with nurses and fellow patients, seeing which books or magazines he is reading, looking on the bedside table for "get well" cards or medications, and noting how much of a meal has been consumed. Although an overview of the patient's appearance is *reported* as part of the physical examination, it can usually be *ascertained* most readily during the interview. Does the patient appear uncomfortable? How are his mood and manner? Does he have abnormalities of appearance that are evident from afar, such as jaundice or the coarse facial features of acromegaly? Do his complaints seem inconsistent with his appearance and behavior? Is the interview frequently interrupted by paroxysms of pain, coughing, or crying?

2. Students should remember that the physical examination is an extreme, though sanctioned, violation of a patient's privacy. Every effort must be made to allow patients as much modesty as possible. Doors should be closed, curtains drawn, and visitors asked to excuse themselves (unless the patient is a child). Portions of the

body should be undraped only for as long as it takes to examine them.

3. Patient comfort, both mental and physical, is of primary importance. The student must let a patient know in advance what she is going to do. She should ask the patient to tell her if he feels too tired or uncomfortable to continue and be ready to postpone the examination herself if it is obviously causing great distress. She should also be sensitive to the fact that certain portions of the examination may be embarrassing or uncomfortable. Statements such as "I know this is going to be uncomfortable for you; I'm sorry" or "This may be uncomfortable; I'll be as gentle as I can" are much appreciated. Particularly unpleasant procedures, such as the rectal examination, may be performed last.

4. Whatever is encountered, the examiner must remain composed, pleasant, and imperturbable. She should not respond to abnormal findings with comments or facial expressions that are likely to upset her patient. She should also refrain from commenting aloud each time that part of the examination is normal. Though this represents an attempt to reassure the patient, it almost always backfires when an abnormal finding is reached.

5. A good examination requires a student's complete attention. Radios and televisions should be turned off and there should be little conversation except for that necessary to comfort a patient or engage his cooperation with position changes. The examiner should perform the review of systems during the examination only when quick "no" answers are expected.

6. Students should try to perform all examinations in a uniform, systematic way to reduce the likelihood that they will inadvertently omit an important component. For their first several examinations, they may find it helpful to refer discreetly to notes that remind them of the desired sequence. Nevertheless, student clinicians should understand that any such sequence is somewhat arbitrary and that no harm will result if they improvise from time to time. Certainly, it is unlikely that a patient will exclaim in disgust, "You fool! You must palpate the precordium before auscultating!"

7. Student clinicians should refrain from being drawn into a physical examination prematurely. If a patient wants to demonstrate a physical abnormality during the interview, the student should assure him that it will be scrutinized carefully during the upcoming physical examination and then proceed with the conversation.

Comparing Results

After completing an examination, students should compare their findings with those of the resident or attending. If there are significant discrepancies, they should always return to the patient and ask to re-perform any section of the physical examination in which their findings differed from those of more experienced clinicians. If they are still unsure, they should ask the resident or attending to demonstrate the controversial points at the first opportunity. It is not uncommon for students to be right in such situations; after all, even though they are less experienced, they generally devote more time to their examinations than do busy residents and attendings. Students should always report their own findings, even if these findings do not agree completely with those of other team members who have examined the patient. They may choose to announce both sets of findings, but it would be dishonest to claim another's results as one's own. If they have omitted something such as the rectal examination in deference to patient comfort, they may certainly explain why and report what others found.

Why the Student Might Want to Videotape the Work-Up

A student spends two hours talking with a patient, asking and re-asking questions until the history is evident in every detail. She determines that the chest pain that led to the patient's admission definitely radiated down his left arm. She informs her attending physician of this fact when she presents the case in attending rounds the following morning. The attending subsequently takes the team into the patient's room for further discussion and, while talking with the patient, asks him whether or not the pain radiated down the left arm. The patient responds with an emphatic "no."

This sort of event occurs at least once in the life of every medical student. A patient often tells different stories to the various people who interview him. Rarely is he deliberately trying to deceive his interviewers. Instead, he may have a faulty memory or have realized that his original answer was wrong only after reconsideration. Attendings know that these reversals are not uncommon, so the student need not fear that the episode reflects badly on her interviewing skills or integrity.

5

Admitting Patients

Call Nights

The call night is the most celebrated experience of medical training, anticipated with eagerness by some and with dread by others. The phrase "on call" actually refers to two different, though related, situations. In its wider use, it describes any clinicians who are responsible for admitting new patients on a given day, whether or not these individuals are staying overnight. On some services, this sort of call is divided into "short call" and "long call," such that members of the short call team admit patients for a specified period of time during the day and stay in the hospital only until their work is done. Those on long call share admitting responsibilities with those on short call for the duration of short call and then assume complete responsibility for any evening and overnight admissions.

In the narrower use, call refers only to those on long call—the people who have the *nocturnal* responsibility for admitting new patients and cross-covering already hospitalized patients who develop problems after their physicians have gone home for the night. Although individuals on long call are usually required to stay in the hospital overnight, sometimes they may remain at home until they are needed. Students on call can learn how doctors establish priorities among multiple competing demands and how they conduct efficient investigations of acute problems. Because there are usually many clinical opportunities from which to select, students should seek the advice of their interns or residents about how they should spend their time on call. In most cases, they should concentrate on the newly admitted patients they have been assigned. The call schedule for students varies among institutions and rotations, but they generally have two to 15 long calls per month.

Clinical Medicine Is a Contact Sport

The medical student's contribution to the admissions process also varies somewhat among rotations and institutions. In every instance, however, it is essential that the student play as active a part in the initial care of the patient as possible. Because new clinical clerks are frequently nostalgic for their established learning routine, they may be tempted to relapse at the expense of their clinical experience. For example, after learning that a newly admitted patient's purported diagnosis is pyelonephritis, a student may choose to go to the library for a comprehensive review of kidney infections rather than to remain on the ward for the admitting history and physical examination. *It is an egregious mistake to forsake clinical experience for a textbook.* The care of the patient will generally provide more long-lasting knowledge than reading alone, and it will enhance the interviewing, examining, and analytical skills that truly define the excellent clinician. Fortunately, for most students, caring for patients is also more enjoyable and rewarding than reading textbooks.

   To gain these benefits, of course, a student must be available for the initial management of a patient. Unlike lectures, admissions come at unpredictable times. A student who is present on the ward when the initial evaluation is undertaken, or who is quickly available by phone or pager, will be rewarded with the opportunity to witness the critical events of clinical medicine as they occur. Though one can begin following a patient after admission, much valuable experience will be lost.

The Student's Role

If a student were working with Voltaire's Dr. Pangloss in the best of all possible worlds, she would have unlimited time to interview and examine a patient independently upon his admission. Then, without referring to prior hospital records, she would attempt to determine his diagnoses and develop a plan for further diagnostic studies and treatment. Finally, she would compare her assessment and plan to that developed by the house staff and attendings. Unfortunately, Dr. Pangloss is no longer an attending physician and this idealized scenario rarely occurs.

Instead, the student usually finds that many factors conspire to limit her ability to work independently with a newly admitted patient. Independent access often requires that a student wait until an intern and a resident (and sometimes an attending) have completed their assessments and certain diagnostic procedures have been performed. After this initial burst of activity, an acutely ill patient may prefer not to repeat a comprehensive interview and examination with a medical student. If so, the student must find an alternate way to become involved in the patient's initial management. For example, she might interview the patient with either the intern or the resident, perform a focused physical examination based on their recommendations (see Chapter 4), and postpone the remainder of the evaluation until later. Under these circumstances, even though the student may initially have limited independent access to the patient, she should still do as much independent *thinking* as possible. There is no shame in arriving at the wrong answer; indeed, the student who does so usually learns more than a colleague who merely mimics the assessment of the intern or resident.

Studies

A student should personally review any studies, such as x-rays, electrocardiograms, and blood smears, at the time of a patient's admission. In addition, the student should perform any simple laboratory tests, such as urinalysis and Gram's stains, whenever possible. Every physician should be able to perform these studies if the need arises, and one often finds that it takes less time to do them oneself than to rely on the busy clinical laboratories.

Admitting Orders

Orders are statements from a patient's physician that indicate the specific nursing, pharmacologic, and laboratory interventions he or she wants for the patient. They may be *written* (communicated through the patient's hospital chart) or *verbal* (transmitted orally to a nurse in person or over the telephone). The method of writing orders varies among hospitals and is therefore best demonstrated to students as they begin clinical rotations at a given institution. In all cases, however, the date and time should be included. At the time of a patient's admission, a complete set of admitting orders must be written. Although the precise content of this set will vary from patient to patient, one can list all the fundamental admitting orders with the mnemonic device "AD CAN PAD FILM" (Table 5-1).

Medication orders must be written with great care to avoid disastrous mistakes. One should adhere invariably to the following rules:

1. The order must be legible; in particular, the numbers should be written neatly to avoid confusion between "0" and "6," "7" and "2," etc.
2. The name of the medication should always be written out completely since abbreviations may be misinterpreted.
3. The route and frequency of dosage must be specified (Table 5-2).
4. One should assume that a decimal point will be overlooked accidentally. Thus, a zero should be placed before a decimal point ("0.125 mg" instead of ".125 mg") to draw attention to it and avoid overdosage. For similar reasons, one should never use an unnecessary zero after a decimal point (write "5 mg" instead of "5.0 mg).
5. The term "units," used to describe dosages of penicillin and insulin, should not be abbreviated "U." The "U" often looks like a zero and "4 U regular insulin" may be misinterpreted as "40 regular insulin."
6. Orders stating that a patient is to have a medication "as needed" or "prn" should always include a maximum dose and frequency so that patients are not given too much ("morphine sulphate, 4 mg IV q4h prn" instead of "morphine prn").

A considerate doctor or student will add "please" now and again when writing orders, especially if the requested action requires an unusual amount of effort, such as calling the house officer every four hours with an update on a patient's urine output. Nurses are

Table 5-1. "AD CAN PAD FILM"
mnemonic device for admitting orders

Admit to service	Name of service and names of attendings/residents with their beeper numbers.
Diagnosis	Primary reason for hospitalization, which should be written out completely without abbreviations or acronyms.
Condition	General estimate of condition, such as "fair" or "critical." "Stable" is not usually informative, as it means only that a patient's condition is not changing significantly. Also, one should use the adjective "good" only rarely; if a patient were in good condition he would probably not require hospitalization.
Activity	The degree to which the medical team wants to restrict a patient's movements—e.g., "bedrest only," "up to the bathroom with assistance," and "unrestricted."
Nursing	Any special instructions to nursing personnel, such as the frequency with which to check vital signs and the frequency and method of dressing changes.
Position	Instructions concerning any special positions the patient should be placed in—e.g., "head of bed elevated 30 degrees," "position patient on left side," "turn patient q3h," or "help patient into chair tid" (see Table 5-2 for abbreviations).
Adverse reactions and allergies	A list of medications to which the patient has had an adverse reaction, along with a very brief description of the reaction itself.
Diet	Instructions for the patient's diet—e.g., "regular diet," "Osmolite via feeding tube at 60 ml/hr," "2 g sodium diet," or "regular diet with 1.5-L fluid restriction."
Fluids	Instructions with regard to fluids given to the patient (IV fluid type and rate, IV catheter care), fluids removed from him (nasogastric tubes, Foley bladder catheters, surgical drains, etc.), and their relative balance (requests for a precise accounting of the daily totals in each category and daily weighings of the patient).
If	Conditions under which the team wants to be called immediately by the nurses caring for the patient—e.g., "Call resident if temperature exceeds 101°, pulse >130 or <50, respiratory rate >35 or <8, systolic blood

Table 5-1 (continued)

	pressure >200 or <90."
Labs	Any diagnostic procedures that the team wants to order, such as laboratory tests or radiologic studies.
Medications	All medications the patient is to receive. For each medication, one must include the full name (no abbreviations), dose, and frequency and route of administration. See Table 5-2 for commonly used terms (many derived from Latin).

Table 5-2. Expressions indicating medication dosing frequency and route of administration

qd	once each day
bid	twice each day
tid	three times daily
qid*	four times daily
q4h	every four hours
prn	as needed
qhs	before bedtime
qod	every other day
qAC	with meals
qAM	every morning
qPM	every evening
IV	intravenously
IM	intramuscularly
SQ	subcutaneously
PO	by mouth
PR	per rectum
SL	sublingually

*Of note, "q6h" is not equivalent to "qid." The former expression means "every six hours, night or day" and the latter means "four times each day during waking hours."

obligated to carry out orders whether or not the orders are phrased as requests, but an occasional "please" or "thank you" is appreciated and contributes significantly to the good relationship between doctors and nurses that is so crucial to effective patient care.

Code Status

Patients are increasingly becoming involved in the decisions about their medical care. In many cases, they have specific wishes regarding which medical interventions they want or do not want. Some patients will relay their wishes in the form of a *living will* or an *advance directive*; others will communicate them verbally to the admitting team. If a patient has not completed an advance directive and is deemed incompetent to make decisions during the hospitalization, his family members or a durable power of attorney for health care may be required to make medical decisions. It is important to address these issues in the hospital record so that information regarding the patient's wishes is available to anyone at any time. A patient who decides that he wants a full attempt at resuscitation in the event of a cardiac or respiratory arrest is said to have "full-code" status. One who does not want such an attempt is said to have "do not resuscitate," or "DNR," status. Strictly speaking, it is probably better to refer to "do not attempt resuscitation" status, as this phrase properly acknowledges that the medical team has full control over only the implementation, and not the success, of resuscitation efforts.

To establish a patient's DNR status in the hospital record, the student or physician should do the following: (1) write a brief note in the progress note section of the chart outlining the conversation or summarizing the advanced directive, and (2) write an order in the chart that includes the patient's name and exact wishes (for example, "Mr. Methuselah desires DNR status—no CPR, intubation, or defibrillation"). An order that does not specify exactly what is meant by "DNR" may lead to confusion during a crisis, and one written without the patient's name may prove disastrous if it has accidentally been entered in the wrong patient's chart. It is a good idea to have a patient, or his surrogate decision-maker, sign the chart note to document that he is in agreement.

Research

After the initial management issues are decided and the patient is "tucked in," the student should take the time to review the relevant issues in a textbook. This review is a vital component of the student's education, and it will also allow the preparation of good oral and written patient presentations.

6

Preparing Oral and Written Presentations

Patient presentations are the way one communicates the facts of a case and the conclusions one has drawn from them. At first, the format may seem arbitrary and awkward, and the whole process may be reminiscent of the sort of dramatic recitations required in English classes. With experience, however, the student will find that an orderly presentation of information is crucial to the efficient communication necessary for good patient care. For example, for a clinician to get the opinion of a consultant, he or she must be able to inform the colleague quickly of the relevant facts. Similarly, a well-structured and complete inpatient or clinic dictation will allow others to participate in a patient's care without having to repeat the full history and physical examination. This chapter outlines the analytic steps important in the preparation of both oral and written presentations.

Beyond the Facts

Students must remember that a presentation is not a reiteration of the history and physical examination as they were done but is instead a deliber-

ately rearranged collection of the most significant information. Of course, a novice will rarely know which facts are significant and which are not. This skill requires experience and knowledge. However, a student clinician can make progress by taking the time to read about a patient's problems before presenting the case. This research will help the student classify the collected data and assemble them into a coherent form. In short, one cannot construct a good presentation without first having done a good assessment.

Any presentation, oral or written, does more than just report data; it reflects the presenter's own evaluation of the case. Students sometimes feel they should try to withhold their impressions entirely until the conclusion of the presentation, so that a listener will be unable to detect bias in their accounts. Even if this were desirable, it would be essentially impossible. As discussed below, limitations of time and audience attention demand that students carefully select which data are included, where they are placed within the presentation, and in what order they are mentioned. These choices are necessarily affected by the student's estimation of what is important, and this is in turn influenced by his or her evaluation of the case. Though a perceptive listener will invariably be able to discern much of the presenter's assessment in this way, students should not worry about introducing undue bias. By following the guidelines outlined in this chapter, they can ensure that listeners are also provided with all the information necessary to form independent, contrary opinions when appropriate.

Though the student's assessment is expected to influence the content and organization of the presentation, he or she should not mention diagnostic conclusions or inferences overtly during the body of the presentation. For example, a student should not say "Mr. Henderson is a 45-year-old man who presented to our emergency room today with new-onset angina pectoris." Instead, she should describe the characteristics of the chest pain and its associated symptoms in sufficient detail that those listening can decide for themselves that the pain represents angina. Similarly, a well-demarcated patch of erythematous, warm, and tender skin should be described as such, not as "a cellulitis."

Classifying Data

Historical Versus Objective Data
The information one collects about a patient may be classified in a

number of ways. The first dichotomy is between historical and objective data. The *history* is the information one usually learns from the patient, including the history of the present illness, past medical history, current medications and allergies, social and family histories, and review of systems. Such topics are classified as history even if one learns about them from a patient's medical records instead of one's own interview. The *objective data* include information that could not normally be obtained from the patient, such as the current physical examination and test results. Sometimes, patients will know from their past interactions with physicians that they have certain abnormalities of physical examination or laboratory testing. In such cases, the abnormalities may be considered part of the history, though they are also classified as objective findings if confirmed by one's own physical and laboratory examination. In any presentation, the historical data precede the objective data.

Polarity and Pertinence

Other important distinctions are made between positive and negative information and between pertinent and impertinent facts. *Positive information* includes anything that is abnormal, whether it is the onset of hematemesis, a cardiac murmur, or an elevated serum uric acid level. Conversely, anything that is normal is considered to be *negative*. *Pertinent facts* are those felt to have a direct influence on the analysis of the patient's chief presenting complaints, whereas *impertinent facts* are those that have no such influence. *Impertinence does not imply unimportance.* It only signifies that a fact, no matter how important, lacks any direct connection to the patient's chief presenting complaints. For example, if a comprehensive interview revealed that a patient with a chief complaint of nasal congestion also had a two-month history of syncopal episodes, one would classify the syncope as impertinent even though it might prove to be of greater consequence than the symptom that prompted the patient to seek medical attention. It would receive substantial attention in the assessment and plan.

The consideration of pertinence and polarity allows data to be classified into one of four categories: *pertinent positives, pertinent negatives, impertinent positives, and impertinent negatives.* One begins evaluating the historical information by listing a differential diagnosis for the presenting complaints and then asking: "Which symptoms, predispositions, or pre-existing conditions would argue for or against each of the diagnoses listed?" With the objective data, the question becomes, "What physical findings or test results would argue for or against each diagnosis?"

For example, consider a 65-year-old man, Mr. Pimble Dogma, with a prior history of chronic obstructive pulmonary disease (COPD), diabetes mellitus, and peptic ulcer disease, who presents to the emergency room complaining of worsening cough and dyspnea. In analyzing his history, one first generates a differential diagnosis, a mental list of diagnoses that might account for his symptoms: COPD exacerbation, congestive heart failure, asthma, pneumonia, lung cancer, interstitial lung disease, and so forth. One then asks which historical information argues for and against each of these diagnoses. A COPD exacerbation, for example, would be supported by a similarity to past exacerbations, a recent discontinuation of medications for that condition, or the coexistence of factors that have in the past triggered exacerbations, such as humidity or upper respiratory infection. A diagnosis of congestive heart failure, on the other hand, would be supported by a history of heart disease, recent increases in sodium or water intake, orthopnea, paroxysmal nocturnal dyspnea, lower extremity edema, or nocturia. Asthma would be suggested by an abrupt onset of the dyspnea, a past history of bronchospasm, or Mr. Dogma's report that he has been wheezing. (Wheezing discovered by the clinician on physical examination is an objective finding, not a historical fact.) A diagnosis of pneumonia would be supported by concomitant fever and chills and by the production of thick, discolored sputum, whereas a pulmonary malignancy would be suggested by an extensive smoking history, a significant nonintentional weight loss, or the presence of blood in the sputum. Finally, a diagnosis of interstitial lung disease would be supported by chronicity of the symptoms and the presence of conditions that predispose patients to interstitial lung disease, such as silica exposure.

Through this process, the clinician generates not only a differential diagnosis but also a list of important *differential questions*. Differential questions are those whose answers guide the analysis by arguing in favor of one or more of the differential diagnoses and against others: Have the symptoms developed gradually or abruptly? Has Mr. Dogma missed any doses of the medications he takes for COPD? Has he had orthopnea? Has fever been noted? The various intersections between the answers to such questions and the patient's actual history define the categories of pertinent positives,

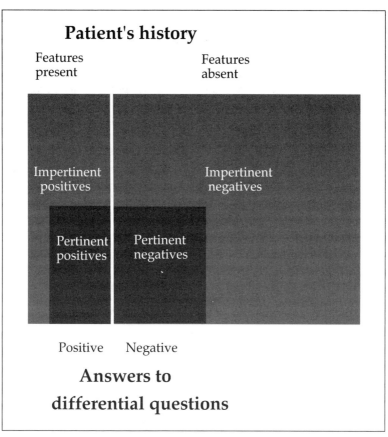

Fig. 6-1. The classification of
historical data by pertinence and polarity.

pertinent negatives, impertinent positives, and impertinent negatives. These relationships are shown schematically in Fig. 6-1. The large rectangle represents the patient's history and is divided into those features that are present and those that are absent. The smaller rectangle combines the affirmative and negative answers to all the differential questions generated by the case.

Pertinent positives are historical features in a given case that are also "yes" answers to differential questions. When discussing Mr. Dogma's history, one would classify the fact that he had a fever to 102° on the morning of admission as a pertinent positive because the presence of fever favors a diagnosis of pneumonia more than heart failure, asthma, COPD, or most types of interstitial lung disease. The fact that his sputum has changed over the last day from thin and clear to thick and yellow-green is also a pertinent positive for the same reason. Because infections commonly exacerbate hyperglycemia in diabetics, a recent worsening in the control of Mr. Dogma's blood sugar levels is a more subtle pertinent positive suggesting pneumonia. In contrast, his 100 pack-year smoking history is a pertinent positive that more strongly supports malignancy, rather than pneumonia, as the etiology of his recent dyspnea and worsened cough.

Pertinent negatives are those features of the history that are not present in the case at hand but that have, because of their absence, the power to narrow the differential diagnosis. That is, they are those "no" answers that enable clinicians to differentiate further among possible diagnoses. The fact that Mr. Dogma has had no prior cardiac disease is a pertinent negative arguing against congestive heart failure. His lack of orthopnea, paroxysmal nocturnal dyspnea, and ankle edema is a pertinent negative that similarly leads one away from the diagnosis of heart failure. The stability of his weight is a pertinent negative that makes malignancy less likely.

Impertinent positives are those historical questions that are answered in the affirmative but do not appear to have direct relevance to the chief complaint. Obviously, one has to know a fair amount about the issues raised by a case to know whether a given fact is pertinent or impertinent, and a beginner will occasionally misclassify a positive because he or she is not aware of a connection between that positive and the presenting complaint. For example, the fact that Mr. Dogma has had a splenectomy might not appear directly relevant to his complaints of dyspnea and cough (that is, it might seem to be an impertinent positive) if one does not know that splenectomy predisposes patients to severe pneumococcal infections, including pneumonia. The importance of research in preparing a presentation should be obvious. It is worth reiterating that impertinence refers only to a fact's relationship to the presenting complaints; many impertinent positives will be of vital importance. Others may be relatively trivial and not merit inclusion in the presentation.

Impertinent negatives are features lacking in the patient's history that do not appear to help clinicians analyze the chief complaint. Mr. Dogma's denial of any abdominal pain, melena, or hematochezia is reassuring, given his past history of peptic ulcer disease,

Table 6-1. Assignment of historical data to various sections of the oral and written presentations

Data	Oral presentation	Written presentation
Pertinent		
Positives	HPI	HPI
Negatives	HPI	HPI
Impertinent		
Positives	PMH, Meds/All, SH, FH, or ROS	PMH, Meds/All, SH, FH, or ROS
Negatives	Not included	PMH, Meds/All, SH, FH, or ROS

Key: HPI = history of present illness; PMH = past medical history; Meds/All = medications and allergies; SH = social history; FH = family history; ROS = review of systems.

but not directly relevant to his present complaints of dyspnea and worsened cough. If he had presented instead with a chief complaint of hematemesis, the absence of these symptoms would be considered a pertinent negative.

Compartmentalizing Data

Classification of historical data into these categories determines where in the presentation they are communicated (Table 6-1); one need not mention the same fact twice. Objective data, whether pertinent or impertinent, are saved for the end of the presentation. This compartmentalization is discussed in more detail in Chapter 7. Though it may seem awkward at first, it does permit an efficient transmission of information and a more cogent and compelling presentation. Eventually, it will become automatic and very much a part of how a student thinks medically.

7

The Oral Presentation

After data have been classified (see Chapter 6), the student is ready to deliver an oral presentation or to compose a written one. Though there is a fundamental similarity between the oral and written presentations, they are discussed separately in this chapter and Chapter 8 to emphasize the ways in which they differ. The oral presentation is discussed first because students often have to give oral presentations before they have had time to sit down and create a written version.

The Pragmatic Presentation

The oral and written presentations have different purposes; therefore, the oral presentation should not be just a recitation of the written version. Written presentations are comprehensive so that they may serve as a sort of "reference book" about the patient. In contrast, oral presentations are for rapid communication (generally less than 10 minutes on an internal medicine service and five minutes on a surgery service) and cannot be overly detailed. If the listeners have questions about data omitted from the presentation, they can always ask for the additional information. Sometimes, even a "standard" oral presentation would be too cumbersome and the listeners will want to hear only a "thumbnail sketch" or "bullet." These terms refer to a very brief synopsis of a patient's story lasting less than one to two minutes and resembling the summary given at the start of the assessment and plan section of the standard presentation (see below).

The format for the oral presentation is outlined later in this chapter. In general, it is best to distribute the information into the sections described below and to follow the expected order of presentation. This rigidity of approach is not intended to stifle creativity; rather, it is designed to allow the efficient transmission of an extremely large amount of information. Because a person listening to an oral presentation does not have the ability to "flip the page" and review an earlier section of the presentation, it is especially important that the information be presented in the expected order. Astute clinicians will occasionally fail to remember a fact from a presentation simply because it was told to them at a time when they were not ready to receive it.

Note Cards

It is certainly permissible for a student to refer periodically to a note card when giving a presentation, especially for exact laboratory values and medication dosages. However, he or she must try to avoid reading from the note card and thus losing eye contact with the audience. Newscasters circumvent this problem by using teleprompters, but these handy devices are not yet available in hospitals and clinics. With experience, students will find that the data fit into some easily remembered patterns and that they have a lessened reliance on their notes.

The First Attempts

Students, even those who have prepared well, will almost always find that their first few oral presentations are awkward and somewhat disjointed. They should not be alarmed. With some practice, the format and style will become familiar and the presentations will

Table 7-1. Physician accomplishments as correlated to performance on first oral presentation

Physician	Accomplishment	First presentation
Hippocrates	Devised oath	Instructor ran upon his sword after suffering through two hours of family history.
René Laënnec	Invented stethoscope	Forgot to report what he heard when he put his ear to the patient's chest.
Robert Graves	Studied exophthalmic goiter	Perceptive listener recorded 357 "uh's" and 96 pauses of five seconds or more.
Sir William Osler	Author of *The Principles and Practice of Medicine*	Concentrated on his note card so intently that he did not notice when the rest of his team left to visit the next patient.

appear more polished. Table 7-1 demonstrates that there is no correlation between the success of one's first oral presentation and subsequent success in medicine.

What to Include

General Principles

After data have been collected, classified, and compartmentalized, the student must still decide which information is significant enough to earn inclusion in the oral presentation, which must be edited, for reasons of clarity and brevity, to a compact collection of the most significant information. There are some general rules about this process:

1. The history of present illness cannot include pertinent positives and negatives for *every* condition in the differential diagnosis. Instead, it should communicate sufficient information to help the listener differentiate among the three or four most likely diagnoses.

2. Impertinent negatives are not mentioned.

3. Almost all services prefer that students shorten presentations by excluding (from the sections that follow the history of present illness) impertinent positives that are not felt to be of great significance. Such deleted information might include elements of the family history, past medical history, and social history (as discussed below).

4. A more controversial issue is whether to delete some of the impertinent positive *symptoms*. Some services, for instance, will want a student to exclude a patient's occasional earlobe pruritus but to mention his periodic crushing, substernal chest discomfort. However, because patients, students, and attendings often differ greatly in their appraisals of a symptom's importance, other services may prefer that a comprehensive presentation include all the impertinent positive symptoms. Residents and attendings will undoubtedly let students know if their presentations include too many, or too few, impertinent positives.

Variation Among Specialties

Presentations vary among services largely because of differences in the approach to the patient. Internists, pediatricians, family practitioners, and other *primary care physicians* generally try to treat all of the patient's current problems and to anticipate and prevent any future difficulties. Therefore, they require more information before deciding on a full course of action and expect a greater degree of detail in the presentations given to them. Gastroenterologists, obstetricians, nephrologists, psychiatrists, and other *specialists* usually focus their attention on one particular current problem and therefore require relatively little information related to issues outside the realm of their specialty. A surgeon hearing about a patient admitted for a hernia repair would likely want to hear only about those past medical conditions that increase the patient's operative risk, such as pulmonary or cardiac disease, or that predispose to certain postoperative complications, such as a history of pulmonary embolism. An obstetrician would of course prefer that the presentations focus largely on gynecologic and obstetric history, and so on. Students should listen carefully to residents' presentations at the beginning of a rotation for an idea of how to structure their own. If there is still doubt, it is certainly appropriate to ask an attending or resident how much detail he or she wants to hear.

Mr. Dogma, the hypothetical patient discussed in this book,

would probably be encountered on an internal medicine service. As a person with multiple past medical problems and a new, undiagnosed problem, he requires a more comprehensive presentation. Students who master this sort of elaborate description usually have no difficulty editing their presentations for other services and should find it relatively easy to give an abbreviated summary whenever appropriate. However, a student who learns only how to give a very brief, undetailed presentation will likely find it difficult to adapt to circumstances requiring a more complete narrative.

Variation Among Cases

Some services most commonly admit patients for whom a diagnosis has already been determined, usually to perform some kind of therapeutic procedure. Such admissions should generally *not* inspire lengthy student presentations packed with pertinent positives and negatives, because almost all the diagnostic and therapeutic decisions will already have been made. For example, if a patient who presented four weeks earlier with cough and dyspnea has since been discovered to have lung cancer and has been admitted for tumor resection, there is no need to set up one's presentation to allude to conditions, such as pneumonia and asthma, that the patient might have had but doesn't. Instead, the relevant differential questions would involve the possible complications of lung cancer, and one would choose pertinent positives and negatives on that basis.

Presenting at the Bedside

In some situations, a student will be asked to give a presentation at the patient's bedside. Although the inclusion of the patient in the audience does not necessitate major changes in the presentation, some modifications should be made in deference to the patient's sensibilities:

1. One should not use expressions such as "Mr. Brudzinski admits to a 120–pack-year smoking history" or "Mr. Brudzinski denies intravenous drug use." Although the terms "admits" and "denies" have no unflattering connotations in the medical dialect students learn, the patient will seldom speak this dialect. To Mr.

Brudzinski, "admit" may imply shame or culpability (his interpretation might be: "Mr. Brudzinski admits to a 120–pack-year smoking history, *so the stupid jerk deserves what he gets*"), whereas "deny" may suggest that his doctors don't really believe his account ("Mr. Brudzinski denies intravenous drug use, *but we all think he's lying*"). One should also avoid phrases such as "Mr. Farnsworth failed chemotherapy," which imply that a bad outcome was the fault of the patient. One might say instead that he *was failed by* chemotherapy.

2. One may want to defer portions of the history that might embarrass the patient, such as the sexual history or an account of alcohol abuse. These facts may be presented after the group has left the patient's room.

3. One should refrain from using descriptive terms in the physical examination that may offend or embarrass the patient. In most cases, the group will be able to observe independently that a patient is obese or appears chronically ill without comment from the presenter.

4. Though it is not realistic to expect the bedside presenter to eschew all medical jargon, an attempt should be made to limit the use of terms the patient does not know. One should also remember that some words, such as "abortion," have a common meaning that is different from the intended medical usage. If a patient seems alarmed by one of these terms, one should pause to correct the misapprehension.

Most patients enjoy bedside presentations of their cases (RM Wang-Cheng, et al. Bedside case presentations: Why patients like them but learners don't. *Gen Intern Med* 1989;4:284–287) and they often interrupt the presentation to make corrections or add detail. Students may be frustrated by such disruptions, but they should never argue with patients or make them feel that the comments are unwelcome. If the interruptions are frequent, the student may assure the patient that his input is important but ask that the remarks be saved until the end of the presentation.

The Presentation Sequence

The rest of this chapter discusses the standard sequence of topics in the oral presentation. Each section contains part of an oral presentation of Mr. Dogma's case along with some instructive commentary. Because the examples are printed in a different typeface, one can reconstruct the full, uninterrupted oral presentation by reading only the paragraphs in that typeface. Chapter 8 includes a full written presentation of the same case for comparison, so that students can see which facts are emphasized in the oral version and which are excluded.

Introduction and Chief Complaint

Each presentation should begin with an "introduction and chief complaint," a succinct statement that gives the listener a basic idea of the acute problem and the medical context in which it has developed. This quick burst of information should include the patient's age, sex, important pre-existing medical conditions, and the primary reason for his coming to medical attention and its duration. It is, in other words, a preview of some of the coming attractions to be discussed more comprehensively later in the presentation:

> Mr. Dogma is a 65-year-old man with a history of diabetes mellitus, chronic obstructive lung disease, peptic ulcer disease, and splenectomy who presents with a two-day history of worsening dyspnea and cough.

Some clinicians feel that the chief complaint should always include a patient's exact words, without any translation into medical shorthand. Whichever words are chosen, the statement should almost always inform the listener about the problem *from the patient's perspective*. One may make an exception to this rule only when there is a reason for hospitalization different from the chief complaint, as happens commonly when patients are admitted for elective procedures or surgeries. Because listeners will always need to know why a patient has been admitted to the hospital, the "chief complaint" in such cases may focus on the reason for admission—that is, *a doctor's perspective*. One then has two options for informing listeners about the actual chief complaint:

1. One may mention it in the introduction and chief complaint section along with the reason for hospitalization. For example, "Mrs. Spubby is a 53-year-old woman with a history of diabetes, hypertension, and cholelithiasis, admitted for elective cholecystec-

tomy, whose chief complaint is a several month history of dyspnea on exertion." The history of her biliary problems and the particulars of her dyspnea would then be presented separately in the history of present illness section.

2. One may consider it an important impertinent positive and describe it in detail in the review of systems. With either approach, the assessment and plan should feature prominently both the reason for hospitalization and the chief complaint.

It is best to refer to people as "man" and "woman" rather than as "male" and "female"; this practice will help the speaker and the audience remember that the patient is a person and not a laboratory animal. For similar reasons, one should refer to a patient by name, not as "the patient." "Mr. Dogma" and "he" take as little time to say as "the patient" does and are much more personal and respectful. It is generally not necessary to include the patient's race in this opening statement because it is only occasionally relevant. If the patient's race predisposes him for one or more conditions in the differential diagnosis, it is classified as a pertinent positive and included in the history of present illness.

Source of History

After the very brief (one or two sentences only) summary provided in the introduction and chief complaint, one describes how the history was obtained and makes an estimate of reliability. Although it is preferable to learn the history directly from the patient, this may not be possible if he has a deficient memory or an alteration in his level of consciousness. In such cases, parts of the story may be provided by family members, close friends, or records from prior hospitalizations or clinic visits. Note that the person providing the history is called an "informant." It is the interviewer, who hears and interprets the story, who is appropriately labeled "historian."

The history was provided by Mr. Dogma and his wife, Velcro. Both appeared to be reliable informants.

History of Present Illness

The history of present illness, or HPI, is the most important part of the history and the section that will most tax one's ability to separate the relevant from the irrelevant and to present facts in a logical order. The HPI is a detailed, chronological account of the patient's experiences from the time when he was last in his usual state of health up to the time that he came to one's attention. Along the way, by mentioning the pertinent positives and negatives for the three or four most likely diagnoses, one ensures that listeners will have virtually all the historical data necessary to analyze the patient's chief complaint. *The presenter's assessment of the case necessarily influences the selection of data for inclusion in the HPI.* Any historical data that are considered impertinent to the patient's chief complaint but are nevertheless important are discussed later in the presentation. Though dozens of equally valid renditions could be constructed, the HPI in this case might be presented as follows:

Mr. Dogma was in his usual state of health until approximately one week prior to presentation, when he noted the onset of rhinorrhea and a mild sore throat. He did not have any fever at that time, nor any change in his usual cough. Over the next four to five days, his symptoms remained stable except that he gradually developed generalized weakness and malaise. One day prior to presentation, he began to notice a change in his cough. The cough, which had been present only in the mornings and had been productive only of scant amounts of thin, clear sputum, became more severe and persisted throughout the day. It also began to awaken him at night. His sputum became thick and more copious and its color changed to a yellowish green. He did not notice any hemoptysis. In association with this change in his cough, Mr. Dogma has had a worsening of his usual dyspnea. Normally, he reports, he becomes short of breath after climbing two flights of stairs, but over the past day he has become dyspneic merely walking to his mailbox. Of note, he had a fever to 102° this morning in association with shaking chills. He has also noted worsened hyperglycemia; despite a decreased appetite, his Chemstrips have been running in the upper 200s instead of his usual low 100s. He denies any orthopnea, paroxysmal nocturnal dyspnea, or ankle edema and has had no known cardiac disease. He also denies any wheezing or chest pain associated with his worsened dyspnea. He has had periodic exacerbations of his chronic obstructive pulmonary disease, at a frequency of about once per year, but believes that his current illness has been different owing to the fever, the more severe dyspnea, and the changes in the quality of his sputum. He denies current "cold" symptoms, headache, stiff neck, photophobia, abdominal pain, vomiting or diarrhea, skin rash, or dysuria. He believes he has received the pneumovax vaccine within the past few years. He has had no recent travel outside of the state, denies recent loss of consciousness or alcohol abuse, and has not come into contact with any pets within the past two months.

This narrative demonstrates three principles of HPI construction:

1. *There can be two layers of "pertinents."* In this case, one group of statements serves to point the listener in the direction of the most likely diagnosis—pneumonia—and a second set helps the listener differentiate among various possible causes for that pneumonia. Mr. Dogma has no travel history that would implicate fungal diseases such as coccidiomycosis (endemic in the southwestern United States), no history of reduced consciousness to suggest an aspiration pneumonia, and no exposure to pets that might predispose him to psittacosis (transmitted by domestic birds). In summary, the HPI has been crafted to point convincingly to a diagnosis of pneumonia without implicating any of the "unusual" pneumonias. One factor, a splenectomy, predisposes Mr. Dogma to pneumococcal pneumonia, the type most commonly encountered in the elderly.

2. *Important pertinent positives beget their own differential questions.* Because Mr. Dogma presented with cough and dyspnea, it was essential to determine that he also had a fever. That fever, a pertinent positive, engenders its own series of differential questions, because fever is compelling support for the diagnosis of pneumonia only if there is no other explanation for it. *Not all pertinent positives require their own sets of "pertinents," only those that are particularly significant and have a number of common causes.* The process is the same as that described earlier. One first makes a mental list of a few causes of fever and then asks what historical features would argue for and against each of them. In this case, the absence of headache, stiff neck, and photophobia has been included as a pertinent negative for meningitis, just as the lack of abdominal pain, vomiting, and diarrhea is a pertinent negative for gastroenteritis. The absence of dysuria makes a urinary tract infection less likely.

3. *One generally tries to group "pertinents" together according to the diagnosis they are supporting or refuting.* In this case, for example, the pertinent negatives for each of the other causes of fever were grouped together, as were the pertinent negatives for congestive heart failure. Moreover, these groupings were arranged in sequence

to answer questions as they might arise in the listener's mind. First, what caused the dyspnea and cough? Second, is there any other explanation for the fever? Third, are there clues as to what kind of pneumonia he has?

In constructing a history of present illness, students may find it difficult to decide how far back in time to start the story. In this instance, it is fairly obvious that Mr. Dogma had a definite change in his status about one week before presentation and that the HPI should begin with this change and then proceed chronologically to the time of presentation. In many cases, however, no sharp transition from "usual health" to "new process" will be apparent, and some or all of the patient's presenting symptoms will be chronic to varying degrees. The student must then form an opinion about which past events or symptoms are intimately related to present ones and designate a starting point for the present illness accordingly. This is a good example of how the organization of an oral presentation must reflect the student's assessment of the case as a whole. Some commonly encountered patterns can be identified:

1. A patient may present with an episode of a previously diagnosed recurring condition, such as asthma, diabetic ketoacidosis, or the painful crisis of sickle cell anemia. In such a case, the underlying condition will have been mentioned in the introduction and chief complaint section. One would then start the HPI with a detailed account of the current episode and then proceed to answer questions about prior episodes taken as a group: When was the first one? When was the last one? How often do they occur? Is there anything that seems to trigger them? Which forms of treatment have been effective in the past? How long do they usually last? Is the current episode unusual in any respect?

2. A patient may present with symptoms that might be related to a previously diagnosed disorder. In such a situation, the decision as to what constitutes present illness is necessarily based on the clinician's assessment of the whole case. For example, a patient with an 18-year history of systemic lupus erythematosis (SLE) who has had, at various times, skin rashes, pleuritic chest pain, arthritis, and seizures may present with abdominal pain and arthralgias. SLE has diverse manifestations and could certainly be causing her current symptoms. If one is sure that it is, then the previous lupus chronol-

ogy may be considered part of the present illness and described after the abdominal pain and arthralgias have been characterized fully. On the other hand, if one feels that the current symptoms are unrelated or is uncertain, the lupus would best be considered past medical history and not present illness.

3. A patient may present with multiple complaints that have evolved independently. The designation of a present illness in such a case can be very difficult, because it may be impossible to discern which complaints are most important and which symptoms are interrelated with respect to cause or time course. If so, the best approach is to discuss the symptoms of each organ system separately within the HPI, tracing each symptom to its inception. In essence, this organization of the HPI is a candid admission that no unifying hypothesis can yet be offered.

Past Medical and Surgical History/Past Surgical History

In the introduction and chief complaint section, which opens the presentation, one provides a *listing* of any important medical problems before describing the symptoms that brought a patient to medical attention. The *details* of all past and present medical problems, however, are saved for the past medical history. This section includes childhood illnesses, adult illnesses (including psychiatric disease), surgical procedures, obstetric history, accidents and injuries, and immunizations. Some clinicians prefer to describe the past medical history and the past surgical history in separate sections. This approach works well also, although it can lead to a confusing fragmentation when one illness has been treated both medically and surgically.

Mr. Dogma's past medical history is significant for diabetes mellitus, which he has had for approximately 11 years. He is now on twice-a-day insulin dosing and has morning Chemstrip measurements ranging between 120 and 150 on average. He has had evidence of mild diabetic nephropathy, with a 24-hour urine in May of last year revealing a protein level of 1.5 g and a creatinine clearance of 75 ml/min. His last ophthalmologic exam was two years ago and revealed mild diabetic retinopathy. Mr. Dogma also has COPD, presumably secondary to his 100–pack-year smoking history. He has been hospitalized twice in the last 10 years for exacerbations and has required occasional steroid courses but never intubation. His last spirometry, three months ago, revealed an FEV_1 of 1.8 liters, an FVC of 3.2 liters, and an $FEV_1\%$ of 56. Mr. Dogma's diagnosis of peptic ulcer disease was made four years ago. Both the gastric ulcer and its subsequent resolution on ranitidine were documented by EGD. Surgical history is significant only for an appendectomy performed over 50 years ago and a splenectomy performed in 1954 after an automobile accident.

Three points should be made about the presentation of the past medical history:

1. Though this section should be as comprehensive as possible in the written presentation (see Chapter 8), time constraints necessitate that it be edited considerably for the oral version. One gives only the most relevant and basic information about the *major* past illnesses. If the patient has an unusually large number of problems, one will have to select the most important for inclusion or risk putting listeners to sleep even before the physical examination is reviewed. As might be expected, the clinician decides which prior illnesses to include largely on the degree to which they help listeners analyze the patient's current problems.

2. Unlike the history of present illness, which is recounted chronologically, past illnesses are usually discussed individually in decreasing order of current importance.

3. One must be careful not to include review of systems data here. Though Mr. Dogma's prior peptic ulcer disease was discussed briefly, one would not mention in this section the current absence of abdominal pain, nausea, melena, or hematochezia. As impertinent negatives, these symptoms would be omitted from the oral presentation.

Medications and Adverse Reactions to Medications

The sections on medications and adverse reactions to them are fairly self-explanatory. When listing medications (prescription *and* over-the-counter), one should remember to use generic names and not trade names (for example, "triamcinolone metered-dose inhaler" instead of "Azmacort") and to include dosages if possible. Also, for patients who have been transferred from other hospitals, it is useful to know the medications the patient was taking at home in addition to those on which he was transferred. When listing adverse reactions to medications, one should describe them in as much detail as possible, because some reactions are more worrisome than others. For example, one might use penicillins, in a pinch, if a macular rash was the only adverse reaction but would not do so if there had been an anaphylactoid reaction in the past.

> Mr. Dogma's admission medications included NPH insulin, 35 units each morning and 15 units each evening; albuterol and triamcinolone metered-dose inhalers at 2 puffs bid; and a multivitamin tablet each day. He reports an adverse reaction only to erythromycin, which produced severe diarrhea.

Family History

As mentioned in Chapter 4, the pertinent information provided in the section on family history generally answers one of two questions: (1) Has anybody else in the family had similar symptoms or a disease of the organ system that is the suspected culprit? (2) Has there been a family history of common diseases that have a significant component of heritability, such as hypertension, diabetes mellitus, breast cancer, and coronary artery disease? As always, pertinent positives and negatives are best included in the HPI and the impertinent negatives can safely be excluded.

> His family history is significant for type II diabetes mellitus in his father and sister. It is otherwise unremarkable.

Social History

When one presents a case to someone who is going to participate personally in the care of a patient, it is helpful to include certain information, whether pertinent or not, that serves as an introduction to the man or woman who underlies "the patient." Though the listener does not really need to know Mr. Dogma's marital status (an impertinent positive) to analyze his presenting complaints of worsening cough and dyspnea, such information helps him convert Mr. Dogma from a scientific puzzle to an actual person. In short, the presentation will be more engaging and effective if a few interesting facets of a patient's life or personality are mentioned briefly.

In the social history, one would also include such things as occupation, occupational exposure, cigarette and alcohol use, recreational drug use, travel history, and so forth. In general, the data fall into one of two categories: (1) a patient's social supports and (2) behavioral factors that increase the risk for particular diseases. Again, pertinent positives and negatives (such as the absence of recent travel) have been transferred to the HPI and impertinent negatives have been deleted.

> Mr. Dogma retired five years ago from his job as a repairman. He is married, lives with his wife, and has one grown daughter. He has smoked two to three packs of cigarettes per day for the last 40 years and uses alcohol only rarely on "festive occasions."

Review of Systems

A complete interview always includes a review of systems (ROS), a catalogue of questions about various symptoms that a patient may have experienced recently. Sometimes, the distinction between past medical history and review of systems can be difficult. For example, if a patient complains of a loss of hearing that has been present for 10 years, should one consider that sensory deficit to be a prior illness (and thus a part of the past medical history) or a current symptom (and thus a part of the review of systems)? One way to resolve this problem is to include such symptoms in the past medical history only if they have been subject to prior medical evaluation and diagnosis. Thus, hearing loss that has never been evaluated would be included in the review of systems, whereas hearing loss known to be from otosclerosis or an acoustic neuroma would be treated as part of the past medical history.

As mentioned earlier, students should try whenever possible to perform a methodical review of systems. After this is done, some reading or discussion with more experienced clinicians will allow them to categorize the answers as pertinent or impertinent and to distribute them appropriately into the various sections of the presentation. Because all pertinent positives and negatives will have been mentioned in the history of present illness, the oral presentation of the review of systems need only include any impertinent positives—that is, symptoms that do not seem to be related to the present illness. Students are reminded that some attendings and residents will want only significant impertinent positive symptoms to be included in oral presentations. It is best to determine their preferences (and their definitions of "significant") at the beginning of the rotation. If there are no impertinent positives, one may quickly say "the review of systems was pertinent only as mentioned in the HPI" and proceed to the physical examination.

> The review of systems was positive for infrequent constipation and occasional lower back pain when lifting heavy objects. Otherwise, it was significant only as mentioned in the HPI.

Physical Examination

Thus far only historical information has been discussed. With the physical examination results, attention shifts to the objective data, which, like historical data, may be classified by pertinence and polarity. The transcript from the oral presentation of Mr. Dogma's physical examination might read as follows:

> On physical examination, Mr. Dogma was an older gentleman, sitting up in bed, in moderate respiratory distress but able to speak in complete sentences. His vital signs included a temperature of 102.6°, a pulse of 116, respiratory rate of 24, and blood pressure of 135/88. His skin exam was unremarkable and he had no lymphadenopathy. HEENT exam was significant only for mild hemorrhages consistent with diabetic retinopathy bilaterally. Examination of the neck revealed no jugular venous pulse elevation. The lung exam revealed symmetrical expansion and mild-to-moderate tachypnea as mentioned above. Fremitus and percussion were normal but auscultation revealed mildly decreased breath sounds diffusely and crackles in the posterior left lower field throughout inspiration. No egophony or bronchophony were present, nor were any rubs or wheezes appreciated. The cardiac exam was unremarkable; specifically, there were no murmurs, rubs, or extra heart sounds. The abdominal exam revealed no tenderness or organomegaly. Vascular exam revealed a right carotid bruit. His extremities were unremarkable; no edema was present. The neurologic exam was significant only for mild loss of pinprick, proprioceptive, and vibratory sensation in his toes bilaterally.

This example illustrates several important points:

1. The description of the physical examination begins with a statement about the patient's general appearance. In a sense, this is the objective equivalent to the brief opening summary made in the

introduction and chief complaint section and it serves to paint a picture of the whole patient for the audience before one proceeds to discuss his component parts separately. It also answers the question "How sick did the patient appear to be?" Note that the patient's age is not included in this description because it is a historical fact and not a physical finding. One can say that someone appears "older" or "elderly" but could not discern the exact age unless informed by the patient or prior records.

2. After this general description, one invariably reports the vital signs at the time of admission. These have a basic importance and should therefore be included in each presentation whether they seem abnormal or not. *All vital signs are either pertinent positives or pertinent negatives.* Indeed, sometimes a "normal" vital sign is really abnormal, such as a pulse of 70 when the temperature is 104° or a pulse of 65 when the blood pressure is 75/40.

3. After the vital signs, one describes each system in turn. Clinicians vary in the order they use, but many prefer to begin with skin, then lymph nodes, HEENT (head, eyes, ears, nose, and throat), neck, thorax, lungs, heart, and so forth. The neurologic exam is generally saved for last.

4. Although most impertinent negatives are omitted from the oral presentation, many clinicians like to hear a quick summary of the heart, lung, and abdominal exams in every case. One must also remember to include negatives that are made pertinent by the diagnostic hypotheses tested in the HPI. For example, in this case the absence of wheezing and pedal edema was mentioned to help refute the diagnoses of bronchospasm and heart failure, respectively.

5. One must remember to refrain from drawing conclusions while relating the physical exam. In this case, for example, one would not want to say that "there were crackles in the left lower lung fields from pneumonia," because the physical examination per se did not tell the examiner that the abnormal sounds were caused by pneumonia. Their putative causal relationship is part of the assessment and is therefore withheld from discussion until after the objective data are presented.

Laboratory and Test Data

The section reporting laboratory and test data should include only the results of tests performed as part of the current work-up, such as the laboratory data collected on the day of a patient's admission to the hospital. Data from past studies are considered part of the history and are therefore mentioned earlier in the presentation if they are important.

> The laboratory data revealed a hematocrit of 35%, an MCV of 82, and a white blood cell count of 18,000 with 80% segs and 11% bands. BUN and creatinine were 25 and 1.3, respectively, and the glucose level was 235. Arterial blood gas analysis on room air showed an oxygen saturation of 88%, PO_2 of 55, PCO_2 of 44, and pH of 7.38. (A PO_2 on room air last year was 75.) Urinalysis revealed 2+ protein but no leukocytes or red blood cells. The EKG showed no Q waves, chamber hypertrophy, or ischemic changes, and the chest x-ray revealed an infiltrate in the left lower lobe without nodules, cardiomegaly, or vascular redistribution. Sputum Gram's stain showed numerous PMNs with many gram-positive diplococci and rare gram-negative rods.

As emphasized in Chapter 5, one should try to perform simple tests (the sputum Gram's stain, for example) oneself whenever possible. Impertinent negatives are again deleted (Mr. Dogma's normal potassium level of 4.1), whereas pertinent negatives (the absence of Q waves on the EKG, which argues against heart failure) and all positives (i.e., abnormal results such as the low hematocrit) are included. It is always helpful to have an abnormal radiograph or electrocardiograph available for review by those who are listening to the presentation.

Summary
One concludes the presentation with a brief synopsis of the most important findings on history, examination, and laboratory testing:

> In summary, Mr. Dogma is a 65-year-old man with a history of diabetes mellitus, COPD, peptic ulcer disease, and splenectomy who presents with a two-day history of dyspnea and a worsening cough productive of thick, discolored sputum. He has fever, left basilar crackles on pulmonary exam, and a left lower lobe infiltrate on his chest film, as well as a leukocytosis of 18,000 with a left shift. The sputum Gram's stain reveals numerous PMNs, many gram-positive diplococci, and rare gram-positive rods, and the arterial blood gas demonstrates moderate hypoxemia worsened from his baseline.

Assessment and Plan

Although one *offers* an assessment and plan at the end of the presentation, it should be clear from the preceding discussion that the student must *perform* the assessment well before the presentation is started. The narrative will be more complete and persuasive if one has a good grasp of the differential diagnosis and the historical and objective clues that help differentiate among the possibilities. In fact, the astute listener should be able to identify much of the speaker's assessment even before the assessment is formally discussed: "Now she's telling me reasons why it does not seem to be heart failure, now I'm hearing things that suggest pneumonia," and so forth.

The assessment and plan section is used to summarize problems, to discuss their possible causes, and to outline a plan for treatment or further evaluation. *Ward team members should not assume that the admitting diagnosis made by the clinic or emergency room physician is correct.* Instead, they should analyze the available information themselves and draw their own conclusions. In many cases, because there will be doubt and disagreement even among experienced clinicians, students may not be able to offer a definitive opinion regarding the diagnosis or treatment of a particular symptom or problem. This is perfectly acceptable, as long as they are prepared to delineate a plan that will reduce the uncertainty. If students are completely baffled, they should find some textbooks that will allow them to suggest some initial management steps. It is not sufficient merely to shift this responsibility to a subspecialty consultation service ("Well, Dr. Kildare, I'm really not sure what's going on. Let's call Endocrinology."). Though consultations play an important part in clinical medicine, in most circumstances they should be obtained only after the ward team has investigated a problem as much as possible on its own and has developed a well-formulated question to pose in the consultation request.

In most cases, the listener (an attending physician, for example) will stop the presentation after the concluding summary and discuss the assessment and plan in a didactic manner (e.g., "So what were you thinking at that point?" and "Which antibiotics would be appropriate?"). Some reading and/or discussion with the resident or intern should allow the student to answer most of the questions asked. Topics likely to come up include (1) the differential diagnosis for the most prominent historical or objective features of the case; (2) which clues in the case argue for or against each diagnosis; (3) the natural history of the suspected disease or condition, including complications; (4) the pathophysiology; and (5) the treatment of the suspected disease or condition. Students should also be prepared to discuss the patient's medications, major past medical illnesses, and the implications and management of any important impertinent positives in the case (for example, Mr. Dogma's carotid bruit and anemia).

Because one almost always discusses the assessment and plan in a question and answer format and not as an uninterrupted soliloquy, a transcript of a full oral assessment is not provided in this chapter. Instead, the reader is referred to Chapter 8, which includes further discussion of patient assessment and an example of a full written assessment and plan for this case.

8

The Written Presentation

As mentioned in Chapter 7, the oral and written patient presentations have different purposes. The oral presentation is designed for rapid communication of the most essential information, whereas the written presentation should serve as a "reference book" about the patient. The major similarities and differences between the two can be summarized as follows:

1. The same format is used for both types of presentation, so that one begins with the chief complaint and then proceeds to give the source, the history of present illness, the past medical history, and so forth.

2. Because the history of present illness must be comprehensive in both presentations, the written version is essentially equivalent to the oral account.

3. The past medical history (PMH) section should be complete in the written presentation though it is almost always edited for the oral version.

4. The written account should include, for the sake of completeness, any impertinent positives that would be omitted from the oral presentation in the interest of time. On some rotations, students will also be encouraged to include as many impertinent negatives as

possible to demonstrate that a detailed interview and a thorough physical examination were undertaken. Residents tend to include many fewer in their write-ups.

5. One should be as specific as possible in describing abnormalities of the physical examination. Diagrams and drawings, even when rendered by those (like me) with a congenital lack of artistic talent, are frequently useful in describing cardiac murmurs and extra sounds, skin lesions, and the exact locations of scars, masses, lymphadenopathy, and tenderness. Simple sketches of radiographs can also be helpful.

6. Unlike most oral presentations, the written presentation must contain an uninterrupted assessment and plan—concise but complete.

7. The written presentation need not be crafted completely in full sentences. Phrases, sentence fragments, and diagrams will suffice for all sections except the chief complaint (CC), the history of present illness (HPI), and the assessment and plan (A&P).

How Many Pages?

There is no "right" number of pages for a patient write-up. The proper length is the one that allows the student to communicate fully but succinctly the facts of the case and the conclusions he or she has drawn from them. Three major factors that influence the write-up's length can be distinguished:

1. *Case complexity*—obviously, patients with elaborate past medical histories and multiple current problems will require a greater investment in pens and paper.

2. *Service*—just as they prefer oral presentations of differing durations (see Chapter 7), different services will expect write-ups of different lengths from their students.

3. *Student handwriting*—students with micrographia will naturally produce shorter write-ups than those who can only fit two or three dozen words on each page. A putative relationship between these three variables and the final write-up length is demonstrated in Table 8-1.

A Few More Words About Penmanship

Some people steadfastly believe that the right to illegible handwriting belongs in the Bill of Rights along with the right to free assem-

Table 8-1. The influence of service, handwriting style, and case complexity on write-up length

C*	Service	Handwriting	Equal length document
1	Internal medicine	Typed	*Hamlet*
1	Obstetrics	Macrographia	Pizza coupon
275	Internal medicine	Micrographia	*War and Peace*
275	Surgery	Macrographia	Gettysburg Address
6	Pediatrics	Micrographia	*The Cat in the Hat*

*Case complexity, which is approximated by the product of the number of prior medical problems and the number of "yes" answers on the review of systems.

bly and the right to free speech. Nevertheless, because patient write-ups have both clinical and legal import, it is essential that they be legible. They are used by the team attending, medical consultants, nurses, and others as the basis for decision making about diagnostic and therapeutic interventions. *They are useless if they cannot be read.* Elegant calligraphy, though appreciated, is not necessary as long as one endeavors to make the handwriting legible.

Special Features of the Written Presentation

The Problem List

Many medical schools prefer that the written presentation include a *problem list*, a compilation of the patient's active medical problems in descending order of perceived importance. "Problem," for this purpose, is defined broadly. It may mean a symptom (for example, dysphagia or chest pain), a predisposition to disease (intravenous drug abuse or a very strong family history of breast cancer), a known illness or condition (asthma or inflammatory bowel disease), or an abnormality of physical examination or laboratory testing (digital clubbing or hypercalcemia). The patient's code status is usually included as well. An example:

Problem List:

1. Chest pain, dyspnea, nausea, and ECG abnormalities = angina
2. Hypokalemia

3. History of asthma
4. Systolic murmur
5. Status-post splenectomy
6. Cigarette use
7. Full code status

Two thorny questions often arise when one is composing a problem list:

1. Does one need to include past problems that are felt to be permanently inactive? The answer is usually "no," unless the past problems predispose to future problems. Thus, one could delete a childhood wrist fracture but would want to list a splenectomy.

2. May one group certain problems together and replace them with a unifying diagnosis? For example, should chest pain, dyspnea, nausea, and ECG abnormalities be listed as separate problems, or should they be grouped together and replaced with "angina?" Each method has its proponents. A convenient compromise is to list such features on one line followed by the proposed unifying label. In complex cases in which there is significant diagnostic uncertainty, it is probably best to list all problems separately.

The Assessment and Plan

Unlike its oral counterpart, the written presentation always requires a full, uninterrupted assessment and plan. This section is essentially an expanded discussion of the problem list, with an emphasis on the proposal of further diagnostic and therapeutic measures (see also Chapter 7). Problems are usually addressed in descending order of immediate importance, with attention focused initially on the differential diagnosis and plan for the complaints that brought the patient into the hospital or clinic. To construct the differential diagnosis, one chooses a small number of particularly important aspects of the case and asks, "Which diagnoses could account for all these features?" (Of course, in some cases, no one diagnosis can explain all the clinical manifestations and one must invoke a second diagnosis. Occam's razor is sometimes a twin-blade.) The other pertinent data of the case are then used to arrange these diagnoses in a rough order of likelihood. In Mr. Dogma's case, the particularly important features might be the cough and worsened dyspnea. The differential diagnosis for these symptoms, as mentioned in Chapter 6, includes chronic obstructive pulmonary disease, congestive heart failure, bacterial pneumonia, interstitial lung disease, and lung cancer. The other aspects of the case, such as fever, sputum production, leukocytosis, worsened hypoxemia, and chest radiograph infiltrates, can then be invoked to justify placing bacterial pneumonia at the top of the list.

The features used to launch this enterprise must be chosen somewhat arbitrarily. The fact that any number of different features, alone or in combination, might serve just as well emphasizes that it is the *process* that is most important. In this example, although the historical features of cough and dyspnea were selected, one could have reached the same final conclusions by focusing initially on many other data combinations: fever, cough, and chest radiograph infiltrates; dyspnea, fever, and leukocytosis; fever, increased sputum production, and worsened hypoxemia; and so forth. Because the facts in this case all point consistently to pneumonia, it is difficult to consider seriously the possibility that the diagnosis might be something else; nevertheless, one must remember that certainty is rarely possible at the time of presentation and that even capable physicians are occasionally fooled by an unusual presentation of a condition not ranked at the top of their differential diagnosis.

The first part of writing an assessment of the presenting complaints consists merely of putting this reasoning on paper. If the existing data seem sufficient, one can state one's diagnostic conclusion and proceed to address other issues, such as specific treatment measures (antibiotics or immunosuppressive agents, for example); important adjunctive, nonspecific therapies (blood transfusions and pain relief); and potential complications (development of deep venous thrombosis in patients whose illness necessitates a prolonged period of bedrest, the induction of angina by a severe upper gastrointestinal hemorrhage in a patient with known coronary artery disease). If the existing data do not allow a specific diagnosis to be made, one should outline a diagnostic plan to reduce the uncertainty and note any interventions that should be made while the results of further diagnostic studies are pending.

After discussing the presenting complaints, one proceeds to comment on any impertinent positives of the case (historical features, physical findings, or lab test abnormalities that are important but unrelated to the chief complaint) and any active medical illnesses. Here, too, one must delineate significance, differential diagnosis, potential complications, and any necessary therapeutic or diagnostic interventions. Finally, one outlines any health care maintenance interventions, such as the ascertainment of cholesterol level and the performance of screening flexible sigmoidoscopy or mammography. It is not necessary to spend a great amount of time discussing problems that are inactive at the time of presentation. For example, Mr. Dogma's quiescent peptic ulcer disease merits only a brief mention in the assessment. Note that some clinicians list the components of the plan together in a single list at the conclusion of the assessment, whereas others prefer to segregate elements of the plan with the individual problems they address.

Diagrams of Convenience

For convenience, many clinicians use diagrams in their write-ups to allow the efficient communication of certain data. These diagrams are by no means standardized, so each student must ascertain whether they have widespread use in his or her institution. One popular diagram of convenience is the *family tree* (Fig. 8-1), which is used in the family history section to show the interrelationships of people and their medical conditions. When the tree is constructed, each individual's medical conditions are written below his or her symbol in the tree. A modest example of Mr. Dogma's family tree is provided later in this chapter.

Simple drawings are also useful for communicating the results of the physical examination. Figure 8-2 shows two schemes that depict the results of reflex testing and the vascular examination, whereas Fig. 8-3 demonstrates a shorthand sketch of a patient's abdomen that can be used when one wishes to communicate the location of scars, masses, tenderness, or organomegaly. Simple depictions of breasts and retinal fundi are straightforward.

One can also use diagrams of convenience to present laboratory data. It is cumbersome to write out the names of the lab tests in addition to the results, so many clinicians use schemes to indicate which tests correspond to which results (Fig. 8-4). In each case, the units of measurement are omitted and must be inferred. For example, a white blood cell count of "6.5" really means "6.5 thousand per mm^3" and a potassium level of "3.9" refers to a value of "3.9 mEq/liter." It is important to note that these "stick diagrams" vary somewhat from institution to institution and that some are not used widely. *To avoid confusion, students should use only those diagram formats that have widespread use within their hospitals.* Note that SGOT

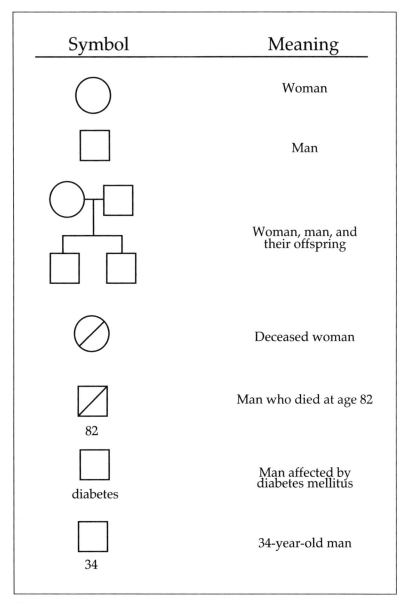

Fig. 8-1. Common family tree symbols.

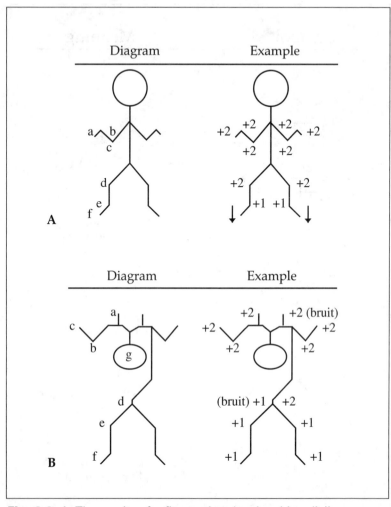

Fig. 8-2. A. The results of reflex testing. (a = brachioradialis; b = biceps; c = triceps; d = patellar; e = ankle; f = toe response.) B. The results of vascular examination. (a = carotid; b = brachial; c = radial; d = femoral; e = popliteal; f = dorsalis pedis; g = the heart.)

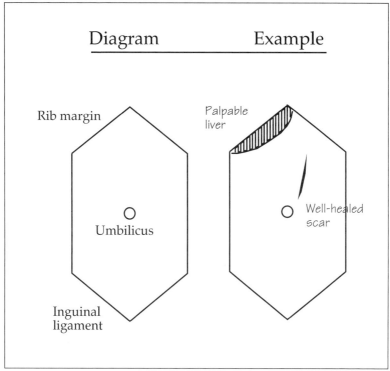

Fig. 8-3. Depiction of the results of the abdominal examination.

and SGPT are also referred to as "AST" (aspartate aminotrans-ferase) and "ALT" (alanine aminotransferase), respectively. Together, they are often called "transaminases."

Honesty in the Write-Up

Because the written presentation is expected to be comprehensive, students may be tempted to make the recorded data appear more complete than those that were actually obtained. Suppose, for example, that a student did not perform complete neurologic or vascular examinations because of time constraints or deference to a patient's fatigue. If she has to compose the write-up before having a chance to resume and complete the examination, the student may be embarrassed about admitting that certain portions of the exami-nation were not performed. She may think as follows: "The vascu-lar and neurologic exams were probably normal, so I'll just write in

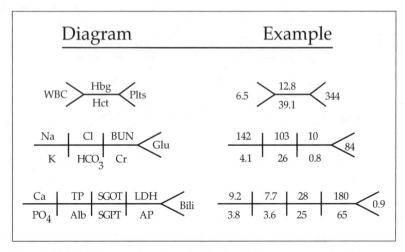

Fig. 8-4. Stick figures for communicating laboratory results. (Hct = hematocrit; Hbg = hemoglobin; WBC = white blood cells; Plts = platelets; Na = sodium; K = potassium; Cl = chloride; HCO_3 = bicarbonate; BUN = blood urea nitrogen; Cr = creatinine; Glu = glucose; Ca = calcium; PO_4 = phosphorus; TP = total protein; Alb = albumin; SGOT = serum glutamic-oxaloacetic transaminase; SGPT = serum glutamic-pyruvic transaminase; LDH = lactate dehydrogenase; AP = alkaline phosphatase; Bili = total bilirubin.)

'normal' or 'nonfocal' and save myself any potential embarrassment." She should derail this train of thought at once. Honest and accurate transmission of data is essential; one never knows when a colleague will refer to the write-up for information about a patient's prior status. If the patient suddenly complains of lower extremity weakness or a cold foot, the student's erroneous descriptions of the baseline neurologic and vascular examinations could prove detrimental to the cross-covering physician's evaluation.

A Lengthy Example

The rest of the chapter will be devoted to a written presentation of Mr. Dogma's case by a student who had a luxurious amount of time with him for interviewing and physical examination. It is in many respects more elaborate and detailed (especially in the assessment and plan portions) than most of the write-ups the student will encounter. The preparation of such a comprehensive write-up, however, is an excellent way for a student to learn and demonstrate that learning. To keep matters simpler for the beginner, an unrealistically small number of acronyms, abbreviations, and diagrams of convenience have been used in this example.

M3 Admission Note

7/29 11 p.m.

CC: Mr. Dogma is a 65-year-old man with a history of diabetes mellitus, chronic obstructive lung disease, peptic ulcer disease, and splenectomy, who presents with a two-day history of dyspnea and worsening cough.

Source: The history was provided by Mr. Dogma and his wife, Velcro. Both appeared to be reliable informants.

HPI: Mr. Dogma was in his usual state of health until approximately one week prior to presentation, when he noted the onset of rhinorrhea and a mild sore throat. He did not have any fever at that time, nor any change in his usual cough. Over the next four to five days, his symptoms remained stable except that he gradually developed generalized weakness and malaise. One day prior to presentation, he began to notice a change in his cough. The cough, which had been present only in the mornings and had been productive only of scant amounts of thin, clear sputum, became more severe and persisted throughout the day. It also began to awaken him at night. His sputum became thick and more copious and its color changed to a yellowish green. He did not notice any hemoptysis. In association with this change in his cough, Mr. Dogma has had a worsening of his usual dyspnea. Normally, he reports, he becomes short of breath after climbing two flights of stairs, but over the past day he has become dyspneic merely walking to his mailbox. Of note, he had a fever to 102° this morning in association with shaking chills. He has also noted worsened hyperglycemia; despite a decreased appetite, his Chemstrips have been running in the upper 200s instead of his usual low 100s. He denies any orthopnea, paroxysmal nocturnal dyspnea, or ankle edema and has had no known cardiac disease. He also denies any wheezing or chest pain associated with his worsened dyspnea. He has had periodic exacerbations of his chronic obstructive pulmonary disease, at a frequency of about once per year, but believes that his current illness has been different owing to the fever, the more severe dyspnea, and the changes in the quality of his sputum. He denies current cold symptoms, headache, stiff neck, photophobia, abdominal pain, vomiting or diarrhea, skin rash, and dysuria. He believes he has received the pneumovax vaccine within the past few years. He has had no recent travel outside of the state, denies recent loss of consciousness or alcohol abuse, and has not come in contact with any pets within the past two months.

PMH: (1) Diabetes mellitus—diagnosed 11 yrs prior to admission. Complications: nephropathy (24-hour urine 5/92: 1.5 g protein & creatinine clearance of 75 ml/min), retinopathy (last ophthalmologic exam 2 years ago: "mild" diabetic retinopathy), neuropathy (numbness bilateral feet for years, no EMG done).

Control: checks sugars bid, usual range 120–150. Hypoglycemic 1–2/month, with palpitations, sweating, malaise.

Meds: Originally glyburide, bid insulin last 5 yrs.

(2) COPD—diagnosed 16 yrs ago, 2.5 cig. packs/day for 40 years, ongoing. Hospitalized for exacerbations '84 & '88 requiring steroids but not intubation. Pulmonary function 4/93: FEV_1 = 1.8 L, FVC = 3.2 L, $FEV_1\%$ = 56, TLC = 6.2 L, RV = 3.0 L, DLCO = 38% predicted.

(3) PUD—in gastric antrum, diagnosed 4 years ago by upper endoscopy after presentation with epigastric pain and guaiac + stool. Treated with ranitidine for 6 weeks with resolution documented on repeat endoscopy.

(4) Chronic eczema—lower extremities, previously treated with skin creams.

(5) Splenectomy—1954 after traumatic motor vehicle accident.

(6) Appendectomy—as teenager.

(7) Health maintenance—uses seat belts, cholesterol level unknown, does not recall vaccination history but no tetanus booster within the last 10 yrs, last stool guaiac test 10 months ago (negative), no screening sigmoidoscopy.

No past history of cardiac, liver, thyroid, or peripheral vascular disease.

Meds: NPH insulin, 35 units qAM
                          15 units qPM
            Triamcinolone metered-dose inhaler, 2 puffs bid
            Albuterol metered-dose inhaler, 2 puffs bid
            Multivitamin, 1 PO qd
            Adverse reactions: erythromycin gave severe diarrhea

Family History:

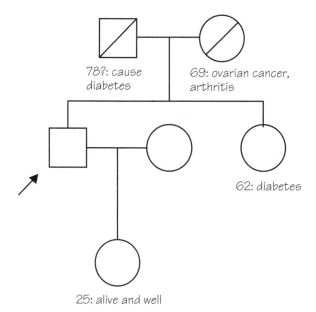

78?: cause diabetes

69: ovarian cancer, arthritis

62: diabetes

25: alive and well

Social History:
> Retired repairman, no known occupational exposures
> Married, lives with wife, one grown daughter
> Smoking history 2–3 packs each day for 40 years, ongoing
> Alcohol use on "festive occasions" only
> 1800 Kcal ADA diet

Review of Systems:
> General: + overall fatigue, fevers and chills (see HPI), no weight or appetite changes
> Skin: no rashes, masses, pruritis, jaundice, or bruising
> HEENT: no headaches, diplopia, visual blurring, tinnitus, epistaxis, sore throat, or hoarseness
> Musculoskeletal: no arthralgias or myalgias except occasional lower back pain with lifting
> Endocrine: no polyuria, polydipsia, voice change, heat or cold intolerance, or change in facial appearance
> Pulmonary: see HPI
> Cardiovascular: no palpitations or claudication (otherwise see HPI)
> GI: + occasional mild nausea and constipation, no abdominal pain, vomiting, diarrhea, melena, hematochezia
> GU: no hematuria, dysuria, urethral discharge, frequency, urgency, dribbling, incontinence, or erectile dysfunction
> Neuro: + numbness/tingling distal feet bilaterally. No depression, vertigo, focal weakness, seizures, vision changes, syncope

Physical Exam:
> General: Older, well-nourished man, sitting up in bed, in moderate distress but able to speak in complete sentences.
> Vitals: T = 102.6, P = 116, RR = 24, BP = 135/88.
> Skin: No rashes, erythema, bruising. + midline abdominal scar, well healed.
> Nodes: No cervical, axillary, epitrochlear, inguinal lymphadenopathy
> HEENT: Cranium normal, hearing within normal limits, external canals normal, tympanic membranes unre-

markable, extraocular movements intact, pupils equal (3 mm), round, and reactive to light; sclerae anicteric, conjunctivae pink, + mild background diabetic retinopathy bilaterally, no sinus tenderness or nasal mucosal hyperemia, oral cavity unremarkable except for poor dentition and numerous filled cavities, no thrush.

Neck: Supple. No thyromegaly or tracheal deviation. No jugular venous elevation.

Thorax: Barrel chest, no gynecomastia.

Lungs: Symmetric expansion and mild to moderate tachypnea, as described above. Fremitus and percussion normal but auscultation revealed mildly decreased breath sounds diffusely and crackles in the posterior left lower fields throughout inspiration. No egophony or bronchophony nor any rubs or wheezes. Forced expiratory time was 5 sec.

Cardiac: Point of maximal impulse nondisplaced, regular rate and rhythm without murmurs, extra heart sounds, rubs.

Abdomen: Mild obesity, bowel sounds present throughout, no tenderness, masses, or organomegaly, liver span 9 cm by percussion in the mid-clavicular line.

Back: No flank or spinous tenderness.

Vascular: All pulses 2+ with normal contours, + right carotid bruit.

GU: Normal male genitalia

Rectal: normal tone, no tenderness, prostate smooth and mildly enlarged, stool neg. for occult blood.

Extremities: No edema, clubbing, cyanosis, synovial inflammation, joint effusions. Full range of motion at all joints.

Neuro:

Mental status: Alert, fully oriented, answers questions appropriately

Cranial nerves: II–XII intact

Motor: Normal tone. Strength 5/5 throughout

Sensory: Intact except for decreased pinprick sensation in distal feet bilaterally and mild, symmetric diminution in proprioception and vibratory sense in the great toe bilaterally.

Reflexes: Brisk and symmetric, no Babinski.

Cerebellar: No dysdiadochokinesia, normal finger-nose-finger and heel-shin testing. No Romberg.

Gait: normal

Labs:

CBC: Hct 35%, WBC 18 K, Plts 300 K, MCV 82, 80% segs, 11% bands. Electrolytes: Na 140, K 4.1, Cl 104, HCO_3 25. BUN/creat: 25/1.3. Glucose: 235. Arterial blood gas (room air): O_2 sat 88%, PO_2 55, PCO_2 44, pH 7.38. (Baseline ABG last year on room air: 94%, 75, 42, 7.39)

Studies:

Urinalysis: dipstick normal except for 2 + protein, microscopic exam showed no leukocytes, red blood cells, casts, or crystals.

ECG: sinus tachycardia, rate 110, normal axis and intervals, no Q waves, voltage changes (suggestive of chamber hypertrophy), or ischemic ST-T wave changes.

Chest x-ray: left lower lobe infiltrate without air bronchograms, nodules, cardiomegaly, or vascular redistribution.

Sputum Gram's stain: numerous PMNs with many gram-positive diplococci and rare gram-negative rods.

Problem List:

1. Dyspnea, worsened cough, fever, leukocytosis, chest x-ray infiltrates, hypoxemia = pneumonia
2. Diabetes mellitus with microvascular complications
3. Chronic obstructive pulmonary disease
4. Anemia
5. R Carotid bruit
6. Peptic ulcer disease—inactive
7. Status-post splenectomy
8. Full code status

Assessment and Plan: In summary, Mr. Dogma is a 65-year-old man with a history of diabetes mellitus, COPD, peptic ulcer disease, and splenectomy who presents with a two-day history of dyspnea and a worsening cough productive of thick, discolored sputum. He has fever, left basilar crackles on pulmonary exam, and a left lower lobe infiltrate on his chest film, as well as a leukocytosis of 18 thousand with a left shift. The sputum Gram's stain revealed numerous PMNs, many gram-positive diplococci, and rare gram-positive rods, and the arterial blood gas demonstrated moderate hypoxemia worsened from his baseline. Individual problems are discussed below in sequence:

(1) Cough and dyspnea—these are Mr. Dogma's presenting complaints. The differential diagnosis for these symptoms is extensive and includes pneumonia, COPD exacerbation, congestive heart failure, interstitial lung disease, and lung cancer. Of these, pneumonia seems the most likely diagnosis by far, given the fever, sputum changes, worsened glucose control, leukocytosis with left shift, worsened hypoxemia, and chest x-ray infiltrate. Infections such as pneumonia can trigger exacerbations of obstructive lung disease, so it is possible that the latter is contributing to the dyspnea and cough to some extent. Nevertheless, the absence of wheezes or marked prolongation of the forced expiratory time on physical exam suggests that his COPD is not significantly worse than baseline. Congestive heart failure is quite unlikely, as Mr. Dogma has no known cardiac dysfunction, no orthopnea or paroxysmal nocturnal dyspnea, no Q waves on ECG, a normal cardiac exam, and no jugular venous elevation, bibasilar crackles, or peripheral edema. The x-ray also failed to show changes consistent with CHF (cardiomegaly, vascular redistribution). There is similarly no reason to implicate interstitial lung disease, given the acute nature of the illness and the type of x-ray changes that are present. He has no illnesses or exposure history that should predispose him to interstitial lung diseases. Pulmonary malignancies must be considered, unfortunately, in anyone with such a significant smoking history, but there is no evidence for one in this case. He has no hemoptysis, weight loss, or digital clubbing, and his chest x-ray reveals no nodules or masses. Of course, it is possible that his left lower lobe infiltrate is "hiding" a lung cancer, and his pneumonia could conceivably be postobstructive in nature (i.e., brought about by a secondary infection of an atelectatic lung distal to a bronchus partially obstructed by cancer). Therefore,

it would be wise to repeat a chest x-ray after the pneumonia is treated to be sure that no masses are present. Since postobstructive pneumonia may fail to resolve until the obstruction is cleared, a lack of response to antibiotics in this case should prompt further investigation, such as chest computed tomography and/or bronchoscopy.

The etiology of Mr. Dogma's pneumonia is most likely the pneumococcus. The pneumococcus is the most common cause of pneumonia in the elderly, and his splenectomy increases his risk for this infection even though he received the pneumococcal vaccination. The Gram's stain showing gram-positive diplococci is strongly suggestive as well. Pneumococci almost always respond to therapy with penicillin, and this would be a reasonable agent to use. Still, because the Gram's stain also showed some gram-negative rods, and patients with either COPD or splenectomy are at risk for <u>Haemophilus influenzae</u>, it might be more prudent to use an antimicrobial agent with a broader spectrum until blood and sputum culture results are available. Cefuroxime, a second-generation cephalosporin, is a good choice because it covers most gram-positive organisms, including pneumococcus, as well as gram-negative organisms such as <u>Haemophilus</u>. With his glomerular filtration rate most recently measured at about 75 cc/min and no change in his creatinine level since then, an appropriate dose of cefuroxime would be 1.5 g IV q12h. Response to therapy can be assessed with the temperature curve, white blood cell count, measured blood oxygenation, and subjective impressions of dyspnea, cough, and sputum production.

Mr. Dogma will also require supplemental oxygen therapy because of his hypoxemia. Unfortunately, his hypercarbia in the face of hypoxemia suggests that he is a CO_2 retainer and may become more severely hypercarbic with oxygen supplementation. Thus, it would be best to begin with a low flow rate of oxygen, such as 1 liter/min, and to repeat the arterial blood gas measurement 30 minutes later to ensure that the hypercarbia has not become severe.

Plan: 1. IV cefuroxime, 1.5 g q12h
2. Blood cultures and sputum cultures (sent)
3. Oxygen at 1 liter/minute with repeat arterial blood gas

4. WBC with differential in AM

(2) Diabetes mellitus—Mr. Dogma has had a typical picture for type II diabetes in that he responded initially to an oral hypoglycemic agent but has since became refractory and required initiation of therapy with insulin. His control on bid insulin dosing has been satisfactory, with glucose levels below 150 most of the time. He gets hypoglycemic approximately twice each month, and it would probably not be wise to try to improve his control with additional insulin at home. His recent worsening of blood sugar levels is consistent with an infection, and he will likely require additional insulin while he is hospitalized. Cautious dosing will be essential; hyperglycemia would impair neutrophil function in the face of an infection, yet hypoglycemia is a risk if too much exogenous insulin is administered while antibiotic treatment brings his glucose control back to baseline. A goal range of 150–250 would be reasonable.

Mr. Dogma has developed three major diabetic complications (nephropathy, neuropathy, and retinopathy), though they are mild in degree. He has not had a recent determination of 24-hour protein excretion, and it would be worthwhile to check one. He might be a candidate for an ACE inhibitor to slow the progression of nephropathy and proteinuria. Mr. Dogma is also overdue for his yearly ophthalmologic examination.

Plan: 1. Continue usual NPH regimen
2. Supplemental sliding scale regular insulin as needed to keep glucose levels below 250
3. 24-hour urine for protein and creatinine clearance
4. Set up ophthalmology follow-up appointment
5. Test dose of captopril after infection cleared

(3) COPD—Mr. Dogma's most recent pulmonary function tests indicate that he has a moderate obstructive defect with significant air trapping. Unfortunately, he continues to smoke. Exam reveals no wheezes at present and his forced expiratory time is at baseline, so it is unlikely that a COPD exacerbation is adding significantly to the respiratory symptoms brought on by his

pneumonia. His arterial blood gas indicates that he retains CO_2, so that it will be necessary to repeat an arterial blood gas on supplemental oxygen.

Plan: 1. Continue current regimen of inhalers
2. Defer steroid therapy at this time
3. Smoking cessation counseling, possible use of nicotine patch

(4) Anemia—Mr. Dogma has a moderate anemia, with a hematocrit of 35%. The MCV of 82 defines it as normocytic bordering on microcytic. No recent hematocrit levels are available for comparison. The differential diagnosis of anemia is vast and includes iron deficiency, marrow replacement or diversion, thyroid and liver disease, renal insufficiency, blood loss, hemolysis, etc. His history of peptic ulcer disease is a risk factor for blood loss, but he has no evidence of occult blood in his stool at present nor any abdominal complaints. None of the other diagnoses appears likely a priori. After a review of the blood smear, the initial work-up should include iron, iron-binding capacity, ferritin, and a reticulocyte count. However, an acute infection decreases the serum iron level and increases the ferritin level, so it is best to wait until the pneumonia is treated before checking them.

Plan: 1. Review blood smear
2. Follow hematocrit qd for 2–3 days while ascertaining WBC
3. Iron, ferritin, iron-binding capacity, reticulocyte count as described above
4. Guaiac stools

(5) Right carotid bruit—Mr. Dogma has no history of stroke and no symptoms suggesting transient ischemic attacks. The natural history of asymptomatic carotid bruits is not well known, but the bruit does suggest the possibility of occult atherosclerotic disease elsewhere—not surprising given his risk factors of diabetes mellitus and cigarette smoking. He should have his cholesterol level ascertained, as this is a potentially remediable risk factor. Smoking cessation, as mentioned above, would be

beneficial. In this setting, an aspirin each day might prove useful for primary prevention of ischemic cardiac and cerebral events.

        Plan: 1. Check cholesterol level
                    2. One aspirin each day

(6) Peptic ulcer disease—There are no symptoms suggestive of recurrence. The anemia is worrisome, however, and if iron deficiency is documented, it will be necessary to look again at the GI tract as the most likely source of blood loss and iron deficiency. Otherwise, there is no indication for intervention at this time.

(7) Health care maintenance plan
           1. Tetanus vaccine
           2. Screening flexible sigmoidoscopy

                    Mary Ann Evans, M3/ *G. Eliot, MD*

An Alternative Approach

The approach used in the preceding example is a traditional one. Some medical schools are now teaching different formats, however, and each student should determine which style is preferred at his or her institution. An alternative format that emphasizes risk factors for disease is taught to students at the University of Michigan Medical School and is outlined below:

1. Source
2. Chief complaint
3. History of present illness
4. Other active diseases
5. Risk factor assessment
    Fixed risks
        Demographic risks (*age, sex, ethnic background, etc.*)
        Genetic risks (*family history*)
  Acquired risks
    Environmental risks
        Occupational history (*exposure to lead, asbestos, etc.*)

        Hobbies
        Travel history
      Behavioral risks
        Substance use and abuse
        Sexual history
      Disease-associated risks (*diseases that increase risks for future problems*)
        Childhood illnesses (*e.g., rheumatic fever*)
        Adult illnesses (*such as heart murmurs, hypertension, prosthetic heart valve, diabetes mellitus*)
      Treatment-associated risks
        Transfusions
        Drug allergies or adverse reactions
        Other (*treatments that increase risk for future problems, such as splenectomy, irradiation, or immunosuppressive therapy*)
    Health maintenance activities
      Disease detection (*breast self-examination, pelvic exam frequency, mammograms, etc.*)
      Disease prevention (*such as seat belt use or dietary habits*)
      Immunizations
      Health promotion (*such as exercise*)

6. Medications
      Prescription drugs
      "Over-the-counter" medications
7. Past medical history (*diseases or problems that are not active, are not a risk for other problems, and are not pertinent to the HPI*)
      Childhood illnesses
      Adult illnesses
      Surgical procedures
      Menstrual and obstetric history
      Psychiatric history
8. Social history
      Personal profile
      Support systems
9. Review of systems
10. Physical examination
11. Laboratory tests and studies
12. Assessment and plan

9

Daily Patient Care

Medical students should know more about their patients than any other member of the ward team. Because they will usually be caring for a smaller number of patients than either the intern or the resident, they will have more time to spend on any given case. For this reason, they should write the daily orders and progress note, acquire the results of diagnostic studies, and participate in the assessment of new problems.

It is even more important that students make an effort to develop true doctor-patient relationships with those for whom they are caring. One of the more frustrating consequences of the first clinical years is a sometimes oppressive sense of ignorance; every day brings reminders of how much one has yet to learn. Fortunately, however, one does not need education or experience to be compassionate, nor any special knowledge to be a sympathetic listener. For this reason, students can be immediately successful at establishing rapport with their patients even if they are baffled by some of the more scientific aspects of medical care. In fact, patients who are not familiar with the hierarchy within teaching hospitals often point to medical students when asked to identify their doctors. In their view, the individuals who have spent the most time talking to and examining them are the ones who deserve the appellation "doctor."

Answering Patients' Questions

Because students typically spend so much time with their patients, they are often the individuals to whom these patients address their questions. Many students find this awkward; they wish to be responsive to their patients' concerns, but they do not feel that they have sufficient knowledge, experience, or authority to answer many of the questions put to them (e.g., "How long will I need to be on this medication?" or "Is there a chance this could mean cancer?"). Students may find the following recommendations to be helpful:

1. If a student does not know the answer to a patient's question, he or she should say so and promise to discuss the issue with the attending and resident. Thereafter, the student or another team member should return with an answer.

2. Responses should be phrased diplomatically and should rarely convey certainty (e.g., "There are many things that might be causing you to be short of breath, Mr. Marlboro, such as pneumonia, heart dysfunction, and lung damage from cigarettes. After we get some tests and talk things over with Dr. Attending, we should have a good idea which of these is the problem").

3. One must beware the tendency to lapse into medical jargon when talking with patients. Such language is likely to confuse and intimidate them (e.g., "Your differential diagnosis includes pneumonitis, CHF, and COPD secondary to tobacco. After the chest film, PFTs, ABG, and CBC, we will decide on a management plan"). Of course, there are some patients who have, or desire, a greater amount of medical sophistication. One can usually detect the level of detail a patient wants to hear and answer accordingly.

Rounds

There are few terms in medicine as ubiquitous as "rounds" and "round." There are also few terms with as many different meanings. In the plural form it is a noun and means "a congregation of medical personnel for a specific purpose." Thus, there are "grand rounds," a large gathering for a presentation; "attending rounds," in which team members meet with the attending physician; and "morning rounds," which are discussed below. Even team social gatherings are sometimes referred to as "GI rounds" or "ethanol rounds."

"To round" is an intransitive verb, which means "to conduct a series of visits in systematic fashion." For example, a student might say "I am planning to round on my patients tomorrow morning at 7:30" or "Yesterday, I rounded so much that I collapsed in a corner and had to be admitted to my own service."

Pre-Rounding and Morning Rounds

Though the exact routine followed by students varies among services and institutions, almost all inpatient services start each day with *morning rounds.* The team briefly visits each patient on the service, discusses any new events or information, and formulates a plan for the day. Students play a key role in this important ritual. Before the start of the rounds, they should quickly check up on each of their patients, a process known as "pre-rounding." They should concentrate on collecting information that will facilitate the efficient completion of rounds, such as a patient's vital signs (including the "T-max," the highest temperature recorded in the preceding 24 hours), morning weight and fluid balance from the previous day, and any events or problems that occurred overnight. A discussion with the nurse caring for a patient is one of the best sources of information; the input of nurses is frequently underappreciated and underutilized. Though interviewing and examining the patient is the important last step, there may occasionally be reasons to refrain from awakening a patient when pre-rounding. In fact, the (not-so-medical) literature offers considerable support for the healing powers of sleep:

> —*the innocent sleep,*
> *Sleep that knits up the raveled sleave of care,*
> *The death of each day's life, sore labor's bath,*
> *Balm of hurt minds, great nature's second course,*
> *Chief nourisher in life's feast—*
> Macbeth II.ii.35–39

Those who doubt this therapeutic effect are likely to alter their opinions following their first nights on call.

Before updating the team on a patient during morning rounds, a student should provide a very brief summary of the case to introduce or re-introduce others to the case before it is discussed. For ht remind those who are not themselves caring for patient from Chapters 6 through 8, that "Mr. year-old gentleman with a history of COPD and diabetes who was admitted with pneumococcal pneumonia three days ago and is now receiving intravenous penicillin therapy." This brief reminder is now the best way to ensure that all team members learn from patients they are not following themselves.

The format for the students' morning rounds presentations differs among services and institutions. In general, one reports any overnight events; updates the team on the most recent symptoms, vital signs, and physical findings; and then briefly discusses the current assessment and plan. For example, after reminding the other team members about Mr. Dogma, the student might proceed as follows:

> Mr. Dogma was mildly nauseated last night for about two hours but felt better by midnight. There were no other problems overnight. He has been afebrile and his morning pulse was 80 with a respiratory rate of 18 and a blood pressure of 140/70. His weight is unchanged at 175 lbs., and his Chemstrips have been 190, 230, 210, and 160.
>
> He is now on day 3 of IV antibiotics for his pneumococcal pneumonia and bacteremia. We are planning a seven-day course of IV therapy followed by a change to oral antibiotics for an additional seven days. Other issues include diabetes, for which he continues on sliding scale coverage with some improvement in his sugars as the infection has been treated, and anemia, for which we are awaiting laboratory evaluation and additional stool guaiac tests. A repeat hematocrit is pending for today.

Orders

Orders are discussed in detail in Chapter 5. Although many orders are written on the day of admission, this set of instructions must be reassessed daily and modified as necessary. It is certainly appropriate for a medical student to participate in writing the orders for a patient, even though they will always require a physician's signature for implementation.

Consultations

A *consultation* is an informed opinion about a patient's care from someone with specific expertise in a given area. For example, a gastroenterologist might be asked to comment on the best approach to investigating a patient's abdominal pain, or a dietitian could be asked to recommend a diet for a patient with renal failure. Consultations can be very useful in clinical medicine, especially for patients with difficult and complex problems. Nevertheless, in most cases, the members of the ward team should try to do as much reasoning and research as possible themselves before requesting a consultation. In so doing, they will maximize what they learn from the case and enable themselves to pose well-formulated questions to their consultants. A consultant can be more helpful if a brief clinical history and particular questions are included in the consultation request, because he or she will then know specifically the issues on which the ward team wants an expert opinion. (The same principle applies to physicians receiving diagnostic study requisitions. The personnel in the radiology department, for example, may choose to modify a study to enhance its sensitivity for whatever finding is suspected by the ward team. Furthermore, the radiologist interpreting the study may be able to make more trenchant observations when he or she knows something of the clinical context.)

Although consulting service suggestions are usually greeted with approbation and gratitude by the ward team, students should remember that they are *recommendations* only. Because the final authority for management decisions rests with the ward team, a student should check with the resident or attending prior to implementing any suggestions offered by a consulting service.

Laboratory Tests

Almost as a reflex, many students and interns order multiple laboratory tests for their patients each morning. Although phlebotomy is a low-risk procedure, it does involve inconvenience, pain, and expense for the patient. Therefore, the student must think in each instance, "How will the result of this test affect my management?" If a test seems very unlikely to influence decisions about the patient's care, it should not be ordered. For example, though it would be appropriate to ascertain Mr. Dogma's white blood cell count peri-odically because it is one of the many clinical indicators of his response to antibiotic therapy, one would not need daily confirma-tion of his normal calcium level or liver enzymes.

Efficiency

Clinical clerks quickly learn that there are some principles of organ-ization that allow them to complete their work most expediently:

1. Perform as much of the day's work as possible in the early part of the day. In particular, the morning is the best time for dis-charging patients, writing orders, scheduling studies, and asking for consultations. Individuals whose assistance is sought will find it easier to furnish the requested service promptly if they are informed early in the day.

2. Keep a list of the things to be done for each patient and cross items off the list when they are accomplished.

3. Use note cards to record the important data for each patient (see Chapter 10).

4. Make as few trips as possible to remote locations such as the laboratories or the radiology department. Advance planning may save time by allowing consolidation of several tasks into each trip.

5. If a test or consultation is particularly important, do not risk losing it in the paperwork maelstrom. Instead, arrange for it over the phone to make certain that it gets done in time.

6. Do not battle obstructionists. If someone is trying to avoid granting what seems to be a reasonable request, one should ask the intern or resident to intervene, thus avoiding both the argument and the waste of time.

7. Do not postpone writing the daily progress note when there is time available early in the day. If significant events occur subse-quently, one can (and should) write an addendum to bring the chart up to date. It may be especially helpful to write a note early if the chart is expected to accompany the patient off the ward for an extended period of time.

8. Obtain the results of laboratory studies as soon as they are available, so that there is plenty of time left in the workday to act on any abnormalities.

9. Never page anyone or risk being put on hold without having

something to work on, such as a progress note or an article. Brief intervals can yield an impressive amount of time if they are added together.

10.   Try to group questions to minimize the number of times the intern and resident must be tracked down. They will appreciate this as well.

Procedures

Many different procedures are performed for hospitalized patients. Some of these are mainly therapeutic, such as intravenous (IV) catheter and chest tube placement, whereas others are chiefly diagnostic, such as lumbar puncture or pulmonary angiography. It is appropriate that students should perform some of these procedures themselves, provided that adequate supervision is available from an intern, resident, or attending physician. (In fact, if the hospital has a phlebotomy service, they may have to make a deliberate effort to obtain the practice necessary to achieve competence at drawing blood or placing IV catheters.) Although students may reasonably expect to perform many of the procedures required by their own patients, they should avoid viewing other patients exclusively as "procedure opportunities." Only under special circumstances should they perform major procedures on patients they have not previously met.

When performing a procedure for the first time, students should always acquire a general knowledge of the technique before entering the patient's room so that only a few comments or suggestions from the supervising physician are needed during the proceedings. Thereafter, whenever performing the procedure, they should review all of its steps in advance to ensure that all necessary supplies have been procured. During the procedure, these supplies generally metamorphose into crumpled paper products, soiled linen, contaminated instruments, and used syringes or needles, collectively known in the scientific community as a "mess." *The safe resolution of such messes is the responsibility of the individuals who have performed the procedure*; nurses are not housekeepers. Students must take special care when handling blood products and needles and should always follow their hospital's hazardous waste disposal policy. In particular, one should refrain from recapping needles after they have been used and should be certain to place all sharp materials in the special container designated for their disposal.

Eventually, students will be permitted to perform certain common procedures, such as phlebotomy and IV catheter placement, without supervision. In difficult cases, they will have to decide how many attempts to make before surrendering and asking for assistance. Although pride may goeth before the fall, in the clinical hierarchy of priorities it cometh after a patient's comfort. Therefore, in general, students should allow themselves no more than two or three attempts before obtaining help. They need not be embarrassed by such an inconsequential and evanescent failure. Rather, they should be proud of their concern for their patients' welfare.

There are many diagnostic procedures students cannot realistically expect to perform, such as cardiac catheterization and esophagogastroduodenoscopy. Students should instead attempt to accompany one or two patients who are undergoing each test to gain an appreciation for how it is done and the degree of discomfort it creates for the patient. At the least, it is important that they see for themselves any permanent record of the results. For example, abdominal computerized tomography (CT) scans and pulmonary ventilation-perfusion ($\dot{V}/\dot{Q}$) scans should be reviewed with a radiologist, and cardiac catheterization films should be viewed and discussed with a cardiologist. Reliance solely on transcribed reports does little to enhance education.

Discharging Patients from the Hospital

Patient discharges are usually accompanied by an abundance of paperwork. Most hospitals have discharge forms that must be completed, and many patients will need prescriptions for the medicines they will take at home (see Chapter 11 for instructions on writing prescriptions). Whenever possible, it is a good idea to complete this paperwork the day before and to write an order in the chart stating that the members of the ward team "anticipate discharge tomorrow." These advance preparations will facilitate the movement of patients into and out of the hospital. If the patient's condition deteriorates, the discharge can always be rescinded.

Medical Records

Medical students play a major role in updating their patients' records daily. These activities, which include writing the team's progress and procedure notes, are sufficiently important to merit their own chapter (Chapter 10).

Unexpected Events

Patients often fail to make the uncomplicated recoveries expected of them. New problems may arise at any time and may provide students with their best opportunities for education and meaningful interaction with patients. Therefore, during the day and on call, it behooves students to remain on the wards as much as possible or to be quickly accessible by phone or pager.

Time Off

Patient care goes on 24 hours each day. Though medical students should be somewhat "possessive" of the patients they are caring for, they cannot be present all the time. In fact, it is important that they attend conferences and have enough time to read about their patients' problems. Thus, when a student has completed the day's work for her patients and all is quiet, she should sign out with her intern or resident. If needed for nothing further, she should leave without guilt. Students are not hospital employees; they are paying tuition in exchange for an education. They deserve sufficient time for reading and relaxation, sustenance, and sleep.

Medical Records

For better or worse, record keeping is an increasingly important aspect of patient care. In the modern medical age, documentation determines reality. If events are not documented, it is assumed that they didn't occur. Although clinicians may sometimes perceive this "charting" to be little more than trivial busywork, some of it is actually important for patient care. This chapter surveys the spectrum of medical documentation and describes the many kinds of chart notes students will be asked to write.

The Chart Is the Official Record

Keeping the Peace

In the right setting, almost any subject can produce controversy. Patient management, as the subject that comes up most often in the hospital, engenders its full share of passionate disagreements. Even when the participants are motivated by a sincere desire to do what is best for a patient, the chart is not an appropriate place for arguments (commonly known as "chart wars"). Can the momentary satisfaction justify the following note?

4/15/94 Renal Consult Note
As I predicted, the patient has gone into acute renal failure

because the wrong antibiotics were prescribed by the ward team. The ongoing use of Lasix is only making matters worse! Perhaps when the patient has to be rushed to the hemodialysis unit they will believe me.

B. Pompous, M.D.

Errors

The hospital chart is a legal document as well as a medical one. Therefore, one should not tamper with or remove any document once it has been placed in the medical record. Mistakes may be crossed out with a single horizontal line (so that they are still legible), labeled "error," initialed, and dated. Even so, one must consider carefully what he or she is writing in order to avoid reconstructed sentences such as this:

error ME 8/2

Mr. Dogma reports that he ~~is having much more trouble breathing than~~ feels great today.

Chart readers will naturally view such a note with a degree of skepticism and concern.

Problem List and Lab Flowsheet

It is crucial that all important information be made part of the permanent medical record, where it can be used by the many individuals who form the current (or future) patient care team. To make sure that the information reaches its intended audience, a student may be asked to prepare and update two aggregations of data within the chart. The first is a *problem list,* which should be placed in a conspicuous location for easy reference. The problem list is essentially identical to the one generated in the assessment portion of the presentation (see Chapter 8) except that it is revised to reflect any new problems that develop during the hospitalization. This list may be lifesaving in the event of a cardiac arrest, because a medical emergency often necessitates prompt action by individuals who are not familiar with the patient. Reference to the problem list allows them to familiarize themselves quickly with the medical context in which the emergency is occurring.

Although most hospitals update their charts daily with computer-generated lab flowsheets, a small number also use a handwritten *laboratory results flowsheet*. This document, which includes laboratory data in tabular form as well as the results of diagnostic procedures, can be a reliable way to dispense important diagnostic data to consultants, nurses, dietitians, and so forth. In addition, the careful compilation of laboratory results on a daily basis makes it easier for the ward team to discern important trends.

Abbreviations and Acronyms

Abbreviations and acronyms are ubiquitous in hospital records and have almost achieved the status of a foreign language. At the start of her ward experience, the typical medical student finds these "conveniences" to be cumbersome obstacles that impede her understanding and make it difficult for her to understand the notes in patients' charts. In response, she may vow righteously never to inflict the same pain on others. Unfortunately, as she becomes more familiar with dozens of commonly used abbreviations and acronyms, she is likely to be seduced into the ranks of the guilty. Anyone thus seduced (I place myself in this category) should compromise by using only well-recognized terms (such as WBC [white blood cell count], IV [intravenous] and DOE [dyspnea on exertion]) and avoiding their more obscure counterparts. Otherwise, one is apt to write something such as:

Pt's SOB and DOE are ↓ed. AF w/ VSS. CXR: LLL ASD s̄ Δ. WBC 11 K ; S/B Cx →GPC c/w PC w/o GNR, will d/c cef. →PCN

which can be loosely translated into English as "The patient's shortness of breath and dyspnea on exertion are diminished. He is afebrile, with stable vital signs. A repeat chest x-ray continues to reveal left lower lobe air space disease without any change from his admission film. His white blood cell count is now 11,000. Because his sputum and blood cultures demonstrated gram-positive cocci (consistent with the pneumococcus) without gram-negative rods, we will discontinue his cefuroxime therapy and institute treatment with penicillin instead." The cryptic nature of the original message is better suited to an espionage novel than to a hospital record. When trying to decode an inscrutable chart note, students should refer to the list of commonly used abbreviations and acronyms in the appendix.

The Daily Progress Note

One of the most important documents in the medical record is the daily *progress note*, which updates a patient's clinical course each day and summarizes the ward team's ongoing assessment and plan. It informs consultants, cross-covering physicians, utilization reviewers, and many others, so its legibility (and that of its author's signature) is essential. Since the medical student should be the person most intimately aware of the patient's status, it is appropriate that he or she be given the responsibility of writing the note each day.

Good progress notes can be written in a variety of styles, and students may find that some services prefer one style or another. Most commonly used is the "SOAP" format, in which the sudsy label is an acronym for "*S*ubjective, *O*bjective, *A*ssessment, and *P*lan." In this scheme, the note begins with a statement of the patient's own (subjective) assessment of his condition. Next, in the objective section, one reports the pertinent physical examination and laboratory findings. Finally, one provides the current assessment and plan as modified by any new developments. For example, Mr. Dogma, the patient from Chapters 6 through 8, might inspire the following progress note on the third day of his hospitalization:

7/31   M3 Progress Note
10:30 a.m.

S: Mr. Dogma feels "a lot better" this morning, and he notes an improvement in his cough and dyspnea. He has not had any episodes of chills since his hospitalization.

O: Vitals: Tm = 99.8, P = 80 , RR = 14, BP = 135/85
Physical Exam:
        Lungs: Fair air flow, inspiratory crackles at left base
           unchanged
        Heart: Regular rate and rhythm without gallops.
        Abdomen: Bowel sounds present. No distention

or tenderness.
        Extremities: No edema present.
Labs: Please see flowsheet. Chemstrips 175/220/180/150
Cultures: sputum—pneumococcus
            blood—pneumococcus
A/P:

1. Pneumonia—Mr. Dogma continues to improve. His symptoms are better, he is now afebrile, and his WBC has improved to 12.6 K. Since the sputum and blood cultures have confirmed the clinical suspicion of pneumococcal pneumonia, we will change our antibiotic coverage from cefuroxime to penicillin. We plan a total of seven days of IV therapy followed by an additional seven days of outpatient oral therapy.

2. Diabetes mellitus—Glucose control has improved with sliding-scale insulin coverage and treatment of his infection. Ophthalmologic checkup scheduled for 8/3, and will begin 24-hour urine collection to quantitate the proteinuria detected by dipstick urinalysis.

3. Anemia—Laboratory work-up still pending. The hematocrit has not changed significantly since admission. One stool has been guaiac-negative.

4. Health care maintenance—Cholesterol level is pending; flexible sigmoidoscopy has been scheduled on an outpatient basis in one month.

Mary Ann Evans, M3/ *G. Eliot, MD*

This progress note illustrates several fundamental points:

1. The date, time, title, and student signature are essential.

2. It is more professional to refer to the patient by name, not as "the patient" or "patient." This practice doesn't take a lot of time, and it demonstrates a greater respect for the individual.

3. The subjective portion should include some of the patient's own words whenever possible, as its purpose is to transmit the patient's point of view.

4. The vital signs are invariably significant and ought to be included each day. A statement that the vital signs are "stable" is not nearly as informative.

5. The documented physical exam may be limited to those areas

made pertinent by the patient's active problems; it is not necessary to include a full examination every day. Thus, a patient with a presenting complaint of right-sided weakness will need frequent neurologic examinations but will not need to have his spleen palpated each day. Similarly, Mr. Dogma deserves a complete pulmonary assessment at regular intervals but would not benefit from (and is unlikely to appreciate) having his gag reflex confirmed each morning. In most cases, one includes a basic assessment of heart, lungs, abdomen, and extremities in addition to whatever other parts of the exam are particularly relevant.

6. Although one will often wish to mention certain laboratory data in the assessment, there is no need to list all of the results if an up-to-date laboratory flowsheet is in the chart. Chart readers can always refer to the latter document. If one does want to include some laboratory data, it is appropriate to use any institutionally preferred diagrams of convenience (see Chapter 8).

7. Because the progress note is focused on "progress," the assessment and plan section includes only problems that are being addressed during the hospitalization. In this case, Mr. Dogma's remote history of peptic ulcer disease, which was discussed only briefly in the admission assessment, does not warrant inclusion in the daily notes. Similarly, the management of the right carotid bruit is not changing day to day and need not be mentioned.

8. In most instances, the progress note may be quite brief. It does not need to be crafted in full sentences as long as it is easily comprehensible.

9. A physician's signature is required on any chart notes that have been written by a medical student.

It is also important to remember that the progress note, like the oral and written presentations, is part of the student's education and should be reviewed with the intern, resident, or attending. Because some physicians habitually sign students' notes without verbal or written comment, a student may have to request feedback about the content of the notes.

Change of Service Notes

One of the most important responsibilities of patient care in a teaching hospital is the *change of service* note. Students, interns, and residents (and sometimes the attending physicians) all follow schedules that call for them to rotate among various services, periodically leaving behind those they have been caring for so that they may take responsibility for a new group of patients. To avoid clinical chaos, such a system must include a way to communicate quickly the essential elements of each case to an individual who has just rotated onto a service and is not yet acquainted with its patients. The change of service note fulfills this role. Although it is usually written by an intern or resident, the note is sometimes delegated to a medical student.

Anyone who is assuming responsibility for a patient's care will eventually need to read the entire chart, or at least most of it. Therefore, the change of service note need not include every detail of the case. Instead, it should contain only the information that will be most useful in facilitating an efficient transfer of care. Since the admission history and physical examination will be available to summarize the patient's status at the time of admission, one needs only to describe the events that have occurred since the patient was hospitalized. The note should always include a list of current medications and inform the new physician of the prior team's plans for investigating and treating each of the patient's problems. A "things to do" list for the first day is very helpful to ensure that nothing important "falls through the cracks." The following is a change of service note that might be written for Mr. Dogma a little later in his hospitalization:

8/4 Change of Service Note
1:30 p.m.

Mr. Dogma is a 65-year-old man with a history of diabetes mellitus, COPD, peptic ulcer disease, and splenectomy who was admitted 6 days ago with a left lower lobe pneumococcal pneumonia. Please refer to the admitting history and physical examination for complete details of his past medical history and presentation. Current active issues include:

1. Pulmonary status—Mr. Dogma's temperature and WBC have been normal for three days. Final blood cultures and sputum culture did confirm the presence of pneumococci. Cefuroxime was started initially for broad coverage of community-acquired pathogens, but on day 3 his antibiotic was changed to IV penicillin. He has tolerated his antibiotics well, and our plan is to complete seven days of parenteral therapy and then

institute oral therapy for another seven days on an outpatient basis. He is now almost back to his baseline level of cough and dyspnea on the same COPD medication regimen he was using prior to admission (see below). He has been weaned off of supplemental O_2.

2. Diabetes mellitus—Initially, glucose control was difficult in the face of the acute infection, but his sugar levels have responded to sliding-scale insulin and the institution of antibiotics. He has been on an 1800 Kcal ADA diet, and today we plan to switch to his baseline insulin dosing schedule. An ophthalmologic examination yesterday showed mild background retinopathy unchanged from his previous examination. Urinalysis shows 2+ protein; 24-hour urine total protein excretion was 2.1 g. Serum creatinine has been stable.

3. Anemia—Mr. Dogma's hematocrit was 35% on admission and his MCV was 82. Work-up to date has included a low-normal iron level (35) and a slightly reduced total iron-binding capacity (250), a ferritin level of 63, three negative stool guaiac tests, and a corrected reticulocyte count of 1.3%. The hematology consult team plans to perform a bone marrow biopsy tomorrow.

4. Health care maintenance—Cholesterol level was 220, with LDL level of 155 and HDL level of 35. Mrs. Minard, the dietitian, has been instructing him about a low-cholesterol ADA diet.

Today's data:
Vitals: Tm = 98.9, P = 74, RR = 14, BP = 128/88
Physical exam:
>Lungs: Fair air flow, continued inspiratory crackles at left base
>Heart: Regular rate and rhythm
>Abdomen: Bowel sounds present. No tenderness or distention.
>Extremities: No edema.

Labs: see flowsheet, please.
Current medications:
>Penicillin G, 600,000 U q12h IV
>Insulin, SQ, 40 units NPH qAM, 19 units NPH qPM
>>10 units regular qAM, 8 units regular qPM
>>Sliding scale (see chart)
>Albuterol inhaler, 2 puffs qid
>Triamcinolone inhaler, 4 puffs qid

Things that need to be done tomorrow:
1. Administer lorazepam at 9:30 a.m.
   before bone marrow biopsy
2. Change to oral penicillin
3. Assess glucose control on home regimen
   being reinstituted today
4. Prepare discharge paperwork and prescriptions
   for the following day

Mary Ann Evans, M3/ *G. Eliot, MD*

Transfer Notes

A *transfer note* must be composed whenever the care of a patient is being assumed by a new service (for example, when a patient admitted to an internal medicine service with abdominal pain is subsequently transferred to the surgery service for an appendectomy). The format is the same as for off-service notes, as one might expect, since in both instances one is communicating the essential details of the case to a physician who is going to assume responsibility for the patient's care. In some cases, however, a transfer occurs urgently and there is little time for writing a comprehensive note. In such cases, one will be able to include only the most important, practical details, such as a list of current medications.

Discharge Notes

The *discharge note* is a brief summary of a patient's hospital course that is written at the time of his discharge from the hospital. It can be considered a transfer note to the patient's outpatient physicians. In most cases, a complete summary of the hospitalization is dictated by the intern or resident, but a student note is sometimes required and always appreciated. One must be careful to keep the note relatively brief, since lengthy, cumbersome notes are seldom read completely. The summary should include a condensed version of the admitting history and physical, the hospital course (with each problem discussed separately), any operations or procedures, discharge medications, discharge diagnoses, disposition (the patient's destination upon leaving the hospital), and follow-up plans (name of the physician(s) who will see the patient after discharge and the appointment dates(s), if available).

Procedure Notes

Significant procedures (almost anything other than phlebotomy or routine IV catheter placement) require documentation in the medical record. Some of these *procedure notes* are described in this section.

Preoperative Note

The preoperative note is usually written on the evening before a planned surgical procedure. First, one describes the procedure and the reason it is being performed (the "indication"). Second, one lists the results of any preoperative studies such as blood coagulation times, chest radiography, and electrocardiography. Finally, one confirms that all the necessary preparations have been made for preoperative orders, blood product requests, and informed consent. For example:

12/29   Preop Note
5:30 p.m.

Planned procedure: Left hemicolectomy
Indication: Biopsy-proven colonic adenocarcinoma at 35 cm
Preop studies:
          Labs—Hematocrit 38%, WBC 11 K, Platelets 335 K, PT 13
                sec, PTT 28 sec
          ECG: Normal sinus rhythm, normal axes and intervals, no
                Q waves or changes of ischemia.
          Chest x-ray: no cardiac enlargement or evidence of
                congestive failure. No infiltrates or nodules.
Preop orders: Written—Nothing by mouth after midnight, 2 g IV
          cefotetan on call to the OR
Type and cross: 2 units of packed red blood cells for procedure
Permit: Signed and placed at front of chart

                              B. Spinoza, M3/ *R. Descartes, MD*

Operative Note

An operative note is written at the conclusion of a surgical procedure and should be a brief summary of the events occurring within
the operating room. Because one of the surgeons will later dictate a
comprehensive note, it is not necessary that the operative note
include every detail:

12/30 Operative Note
11 a.m.

Preop diagnosis: Colonic adenocarcinoma
Postop diagnosis: Duke's stage C2 colonic adenocarcinoma
Procedure: Left hemicolectomy with lymph node sampling and
        exploration
Surgeons: Locke (attending), Descartes (resident), and
        Spinoza (M3)
Anesthesia: General via endotracheal route
Findings: Invasive adenocarcinoma of the left colon with invasion
        through serosa and involvement of sampled lymph
        nodes on frozen section
Specimens: Colon and lymph nodes for frozen (see above) and
        permanent section
Fluid balance: Estimated blood loss 400 cc, 2 L normal saline
        infused
Drains: Jackson-Pratt drain in left lower quadrant
Complications: None
Disposition: Mr. Hume was taken to the recovery room in stable
        condition.

B. Spinoza, M3/ *R. Descartes, MD*

Delivery Note

A delivery note is written after a patient has given birth. The details
vary, of course, with the circumstances of the delivery, but the following information should be included: mother's age, gravida
("G," the number of pregnancies) and parity ("P," the number of
deliveries at more than 20 weeks' gestation) status; prenatal care
and complications; course of labor; description of the delivery; status of the infant (including Apgar scores); use of anesthetics; and
postpartum condition of the mother. The following note might be
written after an uncomplicated delivery:

6/2 Delivery Note
8:30 p.m.

Mrs. Hubbard is a 34-year-old woman, G7 now P7, who has been followed in the obstetrics clinic by Dr. Seuss. Her EDC [estimated date of confinement] was 6/2/93, and her prenatal course was uncomplicated (blood type A+, hematocrit 36%, negative rubella and VDRL). She was admitted 6/2/93 after spontaneous rupture of her membranes at 1:30 p.m. Her cervix was 4 cm on admission and dilated to 10 cm by 6:12 p.m. She was draped in the usual sterile fashion and gave birth to a live 8 lb, 6 oz boy via spontaneous vaginal delivery at 6:20 p.m. Epidural anesthesia and a midline episiotomy were used. Apgar scores were 7 at one minute and 9 at five minutes. Cord blood was sent to the lab and the placenta was expressed intact. The midline episiotomy was repaired with 4-0 nylon suture; restoration of normal anatomy was achieved. The estimated blood loss was 250 ml. Mother Hubbard remains in good condition after the delivery.

M. Sendak, M3 / *Seuss, MD*

Other Procedure Notes

A procedure note is also used to document any nonoperative invasive procedures such as lumbar puncture, thoracentesis, and central line placement. The note should include the indication for the procedure, the method in which it was performed, and any complications:

12/13 Procedure Note
3:15 p.m.
Procedure: Thoracentesis
Indication: Left-sided pleural effusion of unknown etiology
Performed by: Donizetti (resident) and Wagner (M3)
Method: Mr. Gounod assumed a seated position and his left posterior thorax was prepped and draped in sterile fashion. Percussion was used to identify the upper level of dullness, and a site for entry was chosen 2 cm below this point. 1% lidocaine was used for local anesthesia, and then a 2-inch 20-gauge catheter was inserted. 300 ml of clear, yellow fluid was

removed.
Samples: for cell counts, culture, LDH, protein, and cytology
Complications: None. The procedure was well tolerated.
*   Subsequent chest x-ray revealed a decreased effusion with-*
*   out evidence of a pneumothorax.*

R. Wagner, M3/ *G. Donizetti, MD*

Note Cards

Most students find it helpful to keep a private note card of some sort as a record of the pertinent facts about a patient's case. Note cards bolster failing memories and serve as a convenient place to record the varied data generated by a complicated hospital admission. They do have some disadvantages, however. At the time of a patient's admission, they tend to distract students from interviewing and to divert eye contact from patient to clipboard. Moreover, they have a startling proclivity for disappearance, often leaving behind a frustrated student who feels helpless without them. Students are invited to enlarge and duplicate the sample note card provided at the end of this book to determine whether it is helpful.

The front of the card is for documenting the history on admission; the other side has a grid for recording laboratory data and separate spaces for the problem list, the inpatient medications, and test results that cannot be accommodated in the grid. Clearly, any student who wants to include more than a minimal level of detail will find it necessary to develop a miniature version of his or her normal handwriting. One may use abbreviations and acronyms with impunity, as the note card is for personal use and is not intended to be read by others. After the admission data have been recorded, a blank 5 x 7 card should be positioned (with a single staple) atop of the front side so that the bottom and left edges of the two cards are aligned and the back of the card is still visible. This will allow the patient's name, location, and hospital number to be viewed but will also furnish a blank surface on which the student can write information such as vital signs, physical examination changes, tasks to be completed, consult service recommendations, and any study results that will not fit on the back of the card. The two cards may be folded in half for compact storage in a lab coat pocket. This system has a few advantages over some of the others students may encounter:

1. It has a grid to expedite the recording of laboratory data but also recognizes that a note card cannot possibly have prelabeled, dedicated spaces available for every kind of information that may need to be noted. Instead of using an impossibly elaborate note card, the system uses the primary card only for the basic information and adds the smaller white card to achieve the needed flexibility.

2. It allows the student to write in future "to do" lists so that important responsibilities are not accidentally neglected (see the example below).

3. If the patient remains hospitalized and the 5 x 7 card becomes full, it can be detached, turned over, and stapled again for further use.

4. The patient's clinical data and the daily "to do" lists he requires are kept together for easy reference throughout the admission.

Figure 10-1 depicts in miniature the note cards of a student caring for Mr. Dogma as they might appear on August 4, the same day that the change of service note was written. In this case, the student is not rotating off of the service and therefore has written reminders to herself for the next day.

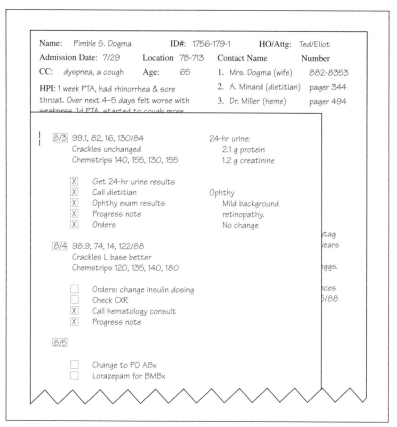

Name: Pimble S. Dogma   ID#: 1756-179-1   HO/Attg: Ted/Eliot

Admission Date: 7/29   Location 7B-713   Contact Name   Number

CC: dyspnea, a cough   Age: 65   1. Mrs. Dogma (wife)   882-8353

HPI: 1 week PTA, had rhinorrhea & sore   2. A. Minard (dietitian)   pager 344
throat. Over next 4–5 days felt worse with   3. Dr. Miller (heme)   pager 494
weakness. 1d PTA, started to cough more.

8/3	99.1, 82, 16, 130/84

    Crackles unchanged
    Chemstrips 140, 155, 130, 155

24-hr urine:
    2.1 g protein
    1.2 g creatinine

[X] Get 24-hr urine results
[X] Call dietitian
[X] Ophthy exam results
[X] Progress note
[X] Orders

Ophthy
  Mild background
  retinopathy.
  No change

8/4 98.9, 74, 14, 122/88
    Crackles L base better
    Chemstrips 120, 135, 140, 180

[ ] Orders: change insulin dosing
[ ] Check CXR
[X] Call hematology consult
[X] Progress note

8/5

[ ] Change to PO ABx
[ ] Lorazepam for BMBx

Fig. 10-1. A miniature representation of M. Evans' note card for Mr. Dogma as it might appear on August 4. The formerly blank 5 x 7 inch card is stapled on top of the front of the patient data card in such a way that important information can be written daily. Note that reminders for the following day have already been added.

Patient Care Off the Wards

Though most of their clinical education is likely to occur on hospital wards, students will have the opportunity to participate in the care of patients in other locations, such as an outpatient clinic, an operating room, a labor and delivery ward, and an emergency room. This chapter provides a brief overview of a student's responsibilities in these settings.

The Outpatient Clinic

Many medical conditions that were formerly evaluated and treated within hospitals are now managed almost exclusively in outpatient clinics. As a result, a clinic may be the only place a student can learn firsthand about the diagnosis and treatment of patients with conditions, such as hypothyroidism and peptic ulcer disease, for which hospitalization is only rarely necessary. In addition, the outpatient clinic is the site where most preventive medicine is practiced—a place where students can learn when to ascertain cholesterol levels or give immunizations. Finally, working in a clinic exposes students to the criteria physicians use when deciding whether to admit a patient to the hospital.

The Outpatient Evaluation

In some respects, a student's interactions with a clinic patient are similar to those with a hospitalized patient. He or she interviews and examines the patient and then discusses (or "staffs") the case with an attending physician or resident. The student and the supervising physician then return to the patient's room together, elicit additional history or physical findings, and conclude the appointment by making recommendations and plans. At the end of the clinic visit (or before the next appointment, if time permits), the student either writes or dictates a note for the patient's medical record. For a patient who is new to the clinic, this note should be similar in content and format to the written presentation of the hospitalized patient. For a patient well known to the clinic who comes for routine follow-up, the note should be more like the daily progress note of the hospitalized patient: a brief summary of the medical context followed by a more detailed account of the issues addressed during the clinic visit. An up-to-date medication list is essential. As always, the note or dictation will require a physician's signature before it can be added to the patient's permanent medical record.

Despite these superficial similarities in procedure, the outpatient setting differs significantly from its inpatient counterpart. Deterioration and progress tend to be less dramatic than on the wards, so even subtle changes may be cause for concern or celebration. In addition, because a patient is in the clinic only for brief, discontinuous intervals, his physicians must consider the implications of their recommendations for the great majority of time in which he is in a world external to their control. A host of questions follow: Can the patient afford this prescription? Is he likely to remember to take 11 medications on four different dosing schedules? Are there stresses at home or psychological factors contributing to his illness? Is the illness causing psychological problems that need to be addressed? Are there ways in which I can help him improve his level of function, even if the cause of his symptoms remains obscure? How will I act on his test results, since they won't be available before he leaves the clinic? What can I do to improve his chances of being healthy five or ten years from now?

Time Management

The outpatient setting has its own pace and requires the skillful management of time. Though students may find it difficult, it is

---

Henry Jekyll, M.D.   DEA no. AU7654321
7829 Hedingham Road
Sylvania, Ohio
555-1233   Refills ___3___

Name   _Robert L. Stevenson_____
Address   _____

  Diltiazem, 60 mg

  Disp: 120

  Sig: 1 (one) PO qid for angina

___Henry Jekyll, MD___   ___3/10/94___
                                          Date

Fig. 11-1. Sample prescription.

important to conclude clinic visits at the appointed time so that subsequent patients are not kept waiting. Therefore, unless a patient has an appointment for a complete examination, one should perform a directed evaluation focusing first on any problems that require immediate attention and then on other issues as time permits. Because the clinic relationship is measured in years and not days, one can always schedule another clinic visit to complete any unfinished, nonurgent business. In fact, a "wait and see" approach can be a great help with confusing problems or vague complaints, provided the patient's condition can tolerate such a delay. At a repeat visit in a week or a month, the situation may be much clearer and allow the pursuit of a more cost-effective work-up. In some cases, the problem will have disappeared even though a "diagnosis" was never made.

Prescriptions
Prescriptions (Fig. 11-1) transmit instructions to a pharmacist about a patient's medications. A student will need to write prescriptions in the outpatient clinic or when discharging patients from the hospital. The prescription must have all the information that the inpa-

tient medication order contains, as well as instructions about the amount of medication to be dispensed and the number of times the medication may be refilled. As always, legibility is crucial. A prescription should contain each of the following pieces of information:

1. Patient's name (and occasionally address).
2. Name of medication. This can be either a generic name or a trade name. In some states, the use of the trade name obligates the pharmacist to dispense the exact brand specified. In other states, the pharmacist can still dispense a generic equivalent unless the physician writes "dispense as written" or "no substitution permitted."
3. Dosage. If a medication is available in more than one dose, it is necessary to specify which one is desired. For example, is it the 0.1-mg size or the 0.15-mg size?
4. Number. Often written after a "#" sign or "disp," this is the amount of medication to be dispensed, specified either by volume (e.g., 50 ml) or number (e.g., 200). Many clinicians write prescriptions that give patients a one-month supply of the medication (so that a once-a-day drug would be numbered "30," a twice-a-day drug would be numbered "60," and so on).
5. Instructions to patient. Often following "sig" (for *signa* or "mark thou"), these instructions inform the patient how often to take the medication and by what route. Some physicians include a brief description of its purpose to help familiarize the patient with the medication. Latin abbreviations (as defined in Chapter 5) are often used, though the pharmacist will translate the instructions into English for the patient.
6. Refill number. Some narcotic prescriptions cannot be refilled.
7. Signature and date. A physician's signature and the date must accompany all prescriptions. In some cases (for example, drugs on Drug Enforcement Agency [DEA] schedule II*), one will need to add the physician's DEA authorization number.

The Operating Room

The operating room (OR) is the natural focal point of surgery services. Medical students should try to participate in surgery as much

---

*The DEA classifies narcotics into separate categories or "schedules" based on their potential for abuse. A DEA authorization number is assigned to physicians in an attempt to minimize illegal access to narcotics.

as possible, particularly on patients with whom they are already familiar. Witnessing a patient's operative procedure is a powerful way to capture permanently the information one has read about a particular surgical condition.

Attire
The operating room, like the Vatican, is more or less an independent municipality within a larger surrounding country. It should come as no surprise, therefore, that customs of dress and behavior there are different from those characterizing the rest of the hospital. Before entering the operating room, surgical teams dress themselves in surgical "scrubs," loosely fitting garments that are laundered after each use to maximize the cleanliness of the operating room. For similar reasons, they put on disposable shoe and head covers and then place masks over their noses and mouths. Bracelets, watches, and rings are not worn in the operating room.

Surgical Nurses and the Sterile Field
In general, by the time a student is ready to enter the operating room, nursing personnel will be there preparing for surgery. There are two types of surgical nurses: *scrub nurses*, who assist the medical team by organizing and dispensing scalpels, suture, and other surgical tools, and *circulating nurses*, who remain further from the operating table and furnish the scrub nurses and physicians with supplies. The circulating nurses are necessary for two reasons. First, they allow the scrub nurses to assist in the operation continuously, and second, they permit the scrub nurses to maintain sterility. Each operation requires a *sterile field*, an environment surrounding the incision that is relatively free of microorganisms, to limit the risk of infection at the operative site. Scrub nurses, like the surgeons and medical students, are part of this sterile field. If they were to get supplies themselves, they would contaminate their hands each time and would be forced to replace their sterile gloves continually. To avoid this inconvenience, they receive any necessary items in a sterile transfer from the circulating nurses, who do not need to keep their hands sterile because they stay far from the operating table.

Preparing the Patient
In many cases, the student will be given the responsibility of preparing the patient for surgery. In general, this "prep" consists of a comprehensive cleansing of a wide area of skin surrounding the

site of the planned surgical incision using soap and disposable sterile sponges. There may be other components as well, such as the shaving of body hair or the insertion of a bladder catheter.

The specifics of technique vary among surgeons. Most prefer that one begin by scrubbing the skin for several minutes with soap solution and a sponge. This cleansing should include an extensive area around the planned incision site; the resident surgeon or attending will provide guidance about the desired boundaries. Next, one places a sterile towel on the scrubbed area, pats the skin dry, and removes the towel by peeling it away carefully by one of its corners. The towel is then deposited in a hamper in such a way that it does not touch either the student or the prepped skin. Finally, one "paints" the exposed skin with povidone-iodine solution (Betadine), starting at the planned incision site and spiraling outward from the center. The sponge should never touch an area twice, and it is important that one not bring the sponge back to the center after it has contacted an area in the periphery. After completing the prep, a student is ready for the hand scrub.

The Hand Scrub

All medical and nursing personnel who will gather at the operating table must wash their hands thoroughly to reduce their bacterial counts. This process, which is known as "the scrub," is not a casual cleansing; rather, it is a formalized ritual in which each part of both upper extremities distal to the elbow is scrubbed with soap and a sterile brush for either a prescribed amount of time or a prescribed number of strokes. The water is controlled by a foot pedal so that the scrubbed hands are not contaminated by the manipulation of a faucet. The preferred method varies somewhat among institutions and is best demonstrated at the start of the surgery rotation; nevertheless, there are some general rules that apply:

1. One should always start the scrub distally and work proximally so that the fingertips and nails are the first areas to encounter a clean brush.

2. One should complete all of the scrubbing one intends to do with a given brush before rinsing off any of the soap with water.

3. When rinsing, one should always keep the hands elevated in such a way that that the "dirty" water drips from the elbows into the sink without touching the hands.

Gowns and Gloves

After the rinsing, the student should back into the OR, keeping his or her hands at chest level in front of the body so that they do not inadvertently touch anything that is not sterile. Once inside the OR, the student should dry the hands with a sterile towel in a distal to proximal direction, being careful not to let the towel touch any clothing. The student then receives a sterile gown from the scrub nurse. These gowns resemble long-sleeved robes, but they are put on "backwards" so that the garment opens across the back with ties hanging loose on either side. A circulating nurse is then asked to tie these strips so that the gown is firmly fastened. (Because the circulating nurse's hands are not sterile, the ties are contaminated in the process. The front of the gown and the sleeves, however, are the important components of the sterile field, and these are the areas the student must be particularly careful not to contaminate.) With the assistance of one of the scrub nurses, the student next puts on a pair of sterile gloves, making sure that the gloves are pulled over the sleeves of the gown to reduce the chance that the sterile field will be exposed to the skin of the forearm. With one newly gloved hand, the student gives the longer of the gown's two front ties to the scrub nurse, who holds it while the student turns 360 degrees. The student then reclaims the tie and fastens it to its shorter counterpart so that the gown fits snugly. One concludes the process by asking the scrub nurse for a damp cloth so that the gloves can be wiped free of any powder that might fall into the surgical site.

The Student's Role in Surgery

Once he or she is in full "battle regalia," the student is ready to participate in surgery. The surgical team first places a series of sterile drapes around the operative site so that only the relevant area is exposed. For procedures that do not involve the patient's head, a drape is usually positioned between the head and thorax to create separate spaces in which the anesthesiologist and the surgical team work. The scrub nurse sets up an equipment tray in a convenient location a short distance from the surgical site. The senior surgeon will tell the medical student what position to take and what to do. In general, students will be asked to help in the retraction of tissues that would otherwise obscure the surgical target site. They may also have the opportunity to help suction blood and to tie and cut sutures. Frequently, during portions of the procedure that require less concentration, the attending surgeon will ask questions about the exposed anatomy, the patient's illness, or the surgical procedure itself. Students will certainly be better able to answer these questions if they have done some reading before coming to the OR.

Maintaining the Sterile Field

The sterile field consists of the scrub nurse's tray, the draped portions of the patient, the gloves of the surgical team and scrub nurse, and the sleeves and fronts of the gowns above waist level. Everything else is considered contaminated, including head covers, masks, and anything below the level of the operating table. After finishing the scrub, the student should not touch anything that is not sterile. Though this edict might seem easy to obey, most will find compliance difficult once they are in the operating room. Actions that usually occur at a subconscious level, such as scratching one's nose, must be pushed firmly into the conscious mind and prohibited.

Inevitably, students will contaminate themselves at least once or twice during their first visits to the OR. The more experienced nurses and surgeons certainly expect this, so one should not hesitate to inform them of any contamination or be embarrassed if they spot a transgression. They will gladly show the student how to restore sterility.

Postoperative Care

At the conclusion of the case, after removing the gown and gloves (gown first, then gloves), the student should help transfer the patient to the postoperative recovery room. There, he or she should offer to write the *postoperative orders* (at most hospitals, all of the orders must be rewritten after an operative procedure), which are similar to admission orders except that they emphasize certain postoperative concerns such as timing of ambulation, analgesia, wound care, pulmonary hygiene, and prophylaxis against thromboembolism. The student should also ask to write the brief operative note (see Chapter 10 for an example). Later, after the patient has returned to his room, the student should perform a brief postoperative assessment to ensure that the recovery is proceeding as expected.

Labor and Delivery

Labor and Delivery Ward

The labor and delivery ward ("L&D") is the focus of each student's obstetrics rotation. Historically, the wards consisted of separate labor rooms and delivery rooms, but the trend recently has been toward the unification of these rooms into specialized suites in which both labor and delivery occur. Cesarean sections are still performed in operating rooms, of course. It is important for each student to remember that, in general, obstetric patients differ from other patients because they tend to be young, healthy women who have been hospitalized only for assistance with a *natural* process. Therefore, the history and physical examination can often be limited almost exclusively to the issues surrounding the pregnancy (see below).

The Mother-Student Labor Union

When a pregnant woman presents to the labor and delivery ward, she is seen initially by a nurse or resident to determine whether admission is appropriate. In some cases, women are admitted to halt premature labor, to replace fluids lost because of hyperemesis gravidarum, or for a planned cesarean section. In the majority of cases, they are admitted for a trial of labor with the expectation of an uncomplicated vaginal delivery.

The assignment of students to cases is done by an attending or resident; some women prefer that no medical students attend their deliveries. When a medical student has been assigned to a case, he should first introduce himself to the woman. He should then take a quick history, emphasizing prior obstetric history (complete information on each pregnancy including gestational age at delivery or abortion, method of delivery, weight of offspring at birth, complications and duration of labor), prenatal care, and prenatal complications. The physical examination should also be brief and may be directed primarily at the abdomen (including fetal heart tones, fundal height, and presentation of the fetus), the heart and lungs, and the extremities (looking specifically for the presence of edema or hyperreflexia). In some cases, the student will be asked to perform a pelvic exam as well (to determine cervical effacement and dilation and the fetus' position and station), though often the supervising resident or attending will instruct him to delete this portion of the examination. After the history and physical examination have been completed, the student may be asked to draw a blood sample to send for cross-matching, in case a blood transfusion is needed at the time of delivery. He should then follow the patient through the many hours of labor, checking on her frequently and providing whatever assistance and comfort he can. The resident, nurse, or attending will perform "cervical checks" on the patient periodically to determine how quickly she is advancing through the various stages of labor. Often, charts monitoring the progress of each patient are posted on a labor and delivery "board" to help the obstetric team monitor the activity on the ward.

The role of the student at the time of delivery varies from case to case. Sometimes, the student will have the opportunity to deliver the baby himself with assistance from the resident or attending physician. In other cases, the student will be the "first assistant" in the delivery. In either case, the student can reasonably expect to participate in the administration of local anesthesia, the delivery of the placenta, and the repair of an episiotomy or any lacerations. A student should not expect to deliver a baby unless he has been actively involved in the care of the mother during labor. The delivery of a baby, though it may be an "opportunity" in the eyes of a student eager for experience, is generally an intimate and monumental event in the parents' lives. It is inappropriate for a student to come in at such a moment as a total stranger to the family.

Postpartum Care

After the delivery, the student should assist in the transfer of the patient to the recovery or postpartum area and should then write a delivery note in the patient's hospital record (see Chapter 10). Subsequently, he should follow the patient until she is discharged from the hospital, watching in particular for complications such as mastitis, uterine bleeding, and endometritis.

The Emergency Room

Visits During Required Clerkships

Few medical students rotate through the emergency room (ER) before their last year in medical school. Nevertheless, students will frequently go there during their required clerkships to perform their initial assessments on newly admitted patients. Emergency rooms are not ideal locations for interviewing and physical examination. They tend to be noisy and full of distractions and often offer little privacy. Interns and residents, because they feel that they must be maximally efficient, are usually willing to tolerate the limitations of ER evaluations. Students should be less concerned about time, however, and are best advised to conduct their full evaluations after the patients have been transported to their hospital beds. Of course, in those cases in which students are not able to pursue the initial work-up independently, they must participate as much as possible wherever possible (see Chapter 5).

The Emergency Room Evaluation

Students doing emergency medicine rotations will find that the initial evaluation of patients who come to an ER is necessarily very different from that of patients in a clinic or inpatient setting. The ER work-up represents the extreme form of the directed interview and physical examination discussed in Chapter 4. Patients must quickly be classified into one of four groups: (1) patients who clearly will require admission but who are medically unstable and therefore need urgent therapeutic interventions such as cardioversion or the initiation of antibiotic therapy; (2) people who have problems sufficiently severe to justify admission but who do not require therapeutic decisions to be made by the ER staff; (3) patients who do not require admission to the hospital but who need follow-up outpatient clinic appointments in the near future; and (4) people who have a relatively simple problem such as a laceration or migraine headache that can be treated primarily in the ER without hospital admission. This sorting of patients by the urgency of their problems, or *triage*, is necessary because sicker patients must be tended to first. Unfortunately, adherence to this principle means that patients with less urgent problems will have to wait even if they arrived first. Most people understand that triage is important and will be patient as long as they are treated with courtesy and apprised of the reasons for any delay.

A good ER evaluation is difficult to perform. In a noisy and hectic setting, one must evaluate patients quickly and yet be sure they are correctly placed into the categories mentioned above. Patient stabilization and triage are more important than diagnostic certainty. The emergency room clinician can remain unsure of a patient's diagnosis, provided that he or she correctly decides whether the problems warrant ER treatment, admission, or outpatient follow-up.

12

Senior Clerkships

Consulting Services

Medical students generally participate on *consulting services* during the last year of medical school; occasionally, they get the opportunity to do consultative rotations amid their required clerkships. A consulting service, which is comprised of an attending physician and one or more residents and medical students, sees hospitalized patients at the request of the ward teams caring for the patients. Generally, the requests are made because teams have questions that require the expertise of the consulting attending. For example, those caring for Mr. Dogma might request an infectious disease consultation to procure recommendations about the best antibiotic to treat his pneumonia. Similarly, a patient who appeared depressed to his surgical team when admitted for a hernia repair might prompt a request for a psychiatric consultation.

The Effective Consultant
Students on a consulting service should try to elicit the patient's history and physical findings themselves whenever possible, instead of relying on the notes placed in the chart by the primary team. In so doing, they will increase their chances of discovering a previ-

ously overlooked piece of information or examination abnormality. Consultants' notes should be brief and to the point, should always include a limited number of specific recommendations, and should be placed on the patient's chart promptly after the consultation request. Notes that are rambling or vague are unlikely to be helpful, in part because they are unlikely to be read. It is often prudent for a consultant to contact the ward team in person or by phone to discuss the case, especially if the consulting service has some recommendations that need to be implemented with urgency.

Learning on a Consulting Service

A medical student who is seeing a patient for a consulting service generally acquires a perspective different from that of a colleague caring for the patient on the ward service. The consultant is able to concentrate on the problems in one limited area and can therefore devote more time to research and rumination than can a student who must simultaneously manage the patient's other medical problems. Unlike the typical ward student, a clinical novice who should read broadly but without extensive depth, a student consultant usually has sufficient background knowledge to read in detail about one or two of the patient's problems. In fact, the student may be asked to obtain recent articles about a given condition or therapy for the ward service (and for the consulting team itself). Despite this focus, the student consultant must not neglect the opportunity to learn from interesting aspects of patient management that fall outside the realm of the consultation. For example, a student asked to provide a gastroenterology consultation for a patient with a possible gastroesophageal reflux may learn more by reading about the patient's history of pulmonary alveolar proteinosis than from the gastroenterology work-up itself.

Consultant Diplomacy

Diplomacy is important when writing a consultant's note in a patient's chart; one must remember that others are responsible for the decisions regarding the patient's care. The following are guidelines that will help ensure that the "consult" does not degenerate into an "insult":

1. Consultants must take care to limit their recommendations to the questions posed in the written consultation (or to their area of expertise, if no specific questions are raised). A gynecology consultant may offend the primary team by making recommendations

about the evaluation of a patient's anemia when asked only for an opinion about uterine prolapse. If consultants want to comment on an issue outside the realm of the consultation, they should contact the team personally and mention their questions or concerns in a courteous way.

2. Consultants should phrase their assessments and recommendations politely. As discussed in Chapter 10, there is no place for inflammatory or argumentative notes in a patient's medical record. If an issue is so important that one is tempted to write such a note, it merits a phone call to the primary team physicians.

3. Unless they have received permission from the primary team, consultants should not write orders in charts or undertake major procedures that have not been requested in the consultation.

4. A consultant should share information with the patient's primary physicians before telling the patient, so that they will not be embarrassed if asked about the issue by the patient. ("What kind of surgery are you going to have? Well, I'm afraid I didn't know you were going to surgery, Mrs. Botticelli.") Unless they specifically defer to the consulting service, ward team members retain the responsibility of imparting bad news to the patient (a disappointing biopsy result, for example).

The Subinternship

A *subinternship* is a rotation in which a senior medical student assumes the role of an intern with close supervision by a resident or attending physician. The subinternship may be in any of several specialities, such as internal medicine, surgery, or pediatrics. A good student—one who tries as much as possible to serve as her patients' primary physician—will find that the responsibilities of subinternship do not differ significantly from those of her required clerkships. For one who has already become accustomed to managing her patients comprehensively, the subinternship will prove different chiefy because her immediate supervisor may be a resident or attending instead of an intern. Two other differences are discussed below.

Write-Ups
Because a subintern acts as a surrogate intern, she is responsible for

writing the "intern admission note" and placing it in the patient's medical record as quickly as possible. This responsibility may force her to compose the note before she has had a chance to research the issues, and it may therefore adversely affect the quality of the write-up. Under such circumstances, the student should read about the various problems presented by her patient at the first opportunity and incorporate her enhanced understanding into the subsequent progress notes.

Signing Out

Whenever a subintern leaves the hospital, she must "sign out" her patients with one of the doctors (usually an intern) on call. The purpose of the sign-out is to provide the cross-covering physician with a brief document outlining each patient's problems and likely difficulties overnight. The transmitted information should include the patient's hospital number and location, whether or not he needs an intravenous catheter, his code status, and any special instructions regarding the work-up of problems that arise during the subintern's absence. If the subintern wants the cross-covering physician to check laboratory results or radiologic studies, she should also try to specify how her team wants him to act on the results. It is best to review the cross-cover sheet with the physician on call in case there are points that are not clear. A subintern's sign-out might read as follows:

Sign-out for Cherie Spino, Purple Medicine Team
Home Phone 678-8899

   1. Bill Roth (1234-567-8)—ward 5C—54-year-old man with a history of HTN, COPD, and CAD admitted 2 d ago with unstable angina. Now pain-free on IV nitro (30 mics) and heparin (900 U/hr) and awaiting cardiac catheterization. Needs IV and full fever work-up. Full code.
**Please check 10 p.m. PTT value in the computer (test already ordered) and adjust heparin drip rate as follows: PTT > 75, reduce to 800 U/hr; 65 < PTT < 75, keep at 900; PTT < 65, increase to 1000 and recheck in 6h.
   2. Frank Infiltrate (8765-432-1)—ward 5C—28-year-old man with paraplegia and urinary tract infection/sepsis. Blood growing out a GNR, not yet fully identified. On ampicillin and gen-

tamicin. Now afebrile but had fever to 102° at 3 p.m. worked up with blood cultures. Needs IV but not a full fever work-up. Full code.

**Please draw a gentamicin trough level at around 11 p.m. tonight (nurse to page you).

3. Ann Hedonia (1564-161-6)—ward 6B—85-year-old woman with CHF and diabetes admitted with CHF flare. Diuresing well on Lasix, 80 mg PO bid and dyspnea improved. Tends to be nauseated after receiving her potassium supplements. No IV. Full fever work-up. DNR status.

The subintern should contact the cross-covering physician upon returning to the hospital to receive an update on any events that occurred while she was away.

Professional Standards

or

Some Anticipatory Preaching

Physicians are entrusted with information that most people share with nobody else. They are also allowed to examine these people in ways that would meet the legal definition of assault in another context. In exchange for these privileges, they must be willing to hold themselves to a certain standard of behavior. The application of this standard antedates the medical degree and salary, coming instead with a student's first experiences in clinical medicine. Some important components of the standard are discussed below.

It is difficult to write about this subject without appearing sanctimonious and judgmental. I am not claiming any moral superiority, and I do not pretend to be the ultimate arbiter of what is right and wrong. Certainly, the principles espoused in this chapter are neither universally accepted nor universally followed. Students will have to decide for themselves whether they are important. Those who do subscribe to their importance may sometimes be disappointed in their own behavior or the actions of fellow students, residents, and attendings. *The demands of patient care can cause all of us to lose sight of issues that are not overtly medical in nature.* Students should try to do what they feel to be right even if they do not have an example set before them.

Courtesy

Certain fundamental rules of etiquette are too often neglected in the turbulence surrounding acute illness:

1. One should knock before entering a patient's room and, once inside, should take the time to introduce oneself both to the patient and to any visitors who are present. When the entire ward team comes in to see a patient for the first time, members with whom the patient is unfamiliar should be introduced.

2. One should not bring food or drink into patients' rooms, even if one feels that it will be very difficult to get through morning rounds without a little coffee. These items should be consumed in the hallways or conference rooms.

3. One must avoid the tendency to lapse into impersonal clinical discussions with other members of the ward team while standing inside a patient's room. Most people do not like to hear themselves referred to in the third person. Moreover, no words should be spoken immediately outside a patient's door that one would not want him to hear. Assume that unconscious or demented patients are able to comprehend and remember what is said in their presence.

4. When conducting an examination, one should obtain as much privacy for the patient as possible under the circumstances. Unless the patient is a child, visitors should politely be asked to excuse themselves temporarily. (If the patient prefers that his visitors stay, he will interject that preference. If one asks him, in the presence of his company, if he wants them to leave, he may feel compelled to say "no" because he does not want to insult them.)

5. One must attempt to be punctual and apologize when late. There are certainly some delays that are unavoidable when one has a busy outpatient schedule or inpatient service, but one should never *plan* to keep patients waiting. If a student has seen a patient in a clinic and is waiting to "staff" the case with a currently unavailable resident or attending, she should periodically return to the patient's room to let him know that he has not been forgotten. Most people will tolerate being kept waiting to a remarkable degree if there is a sincere apology for the delay.

6. If one is going to review a patient's medical record (see Chapter 5), it should be done before, not during, the interview. One may quickly look up a laboratory result or confirm a date, but extensive reading is discouraged. The patient deserves, and effective medical practice demands, eye contact and attention.

7. One should expressly invite a patient's questions.

Confidentiality

Students (as well as residents and attendings) spend so much time talking about patients and their problems that they sometimes forget that such conversations contain private information. Confidentiality is of paramount importance in clinical medicine. For this reason, elevators, cafeteria tables, and stairwells are not appropriate places for medical communication.

Honesty

A student should never introduce herself as "doctor." If a well-meaning colleague (often a resident or an attending) introduces her this way, the student should remember to explain her actual role to the patient privately at the first opportunity. Whatever someone's motive, there can hardly be justification for a deliberate deception of the patient. Most patients are happy to have a medical student helping to care for them; the few who are not deserve respect for their decision. Because most nurses are women, female students may find that the term "student doctor" is preferable to "medical student" in helping patients differentiate them from nurses and nursing students.

Respect

All members of the medical team should treat their patients with respect:

1. One should address any adult patient by title and surname

unless instructed otherwise by the patient. In presentations, even when the patient is not a member of the audience, he should be referred to by name, not as "the patient." Though some believe that the substitution of "the patient" for "Mr. Dogma" and "65-year-old white male" for "65-year-old man" creates an "objective scientific tone" for the discussion, many others would argue that these expressions are needlessly impersonal and ultimately belie the humane goals of clinical medicine. Mr. Dogma is a *person* with certain medical problems, not a mere conglomeration of scientific data.

2. One must respect a patient's autonomy and put forth every effort to give him as much control as possible. One of the many disabling features of illness is its tendency to make people feel that they no longer have any input into the decisions about their lives. To ameliorate this sense of lost control, one should ask, "May I draw a blood sample?" rather than say, "You have to have a blood draw" or "I need to draw some blood." Similarly, when possible, one should always notify a patient before a procedure takes place so that he may plan for it and will not be taken by surprise. Out of respect for his autonomy, the patient should be asked to uncover an area for examination or to give permission for the examiner to do it. If the examination requires at some point that he change his position, he should be allowed to do so himself. One may offer assistance but should not manipulate him without permission.

3. Though it may prove very difficult, one should refrain from making patients the objects of private humor. Without question, team morale is boosted by lightheartedness, and it is true that laughter makes a stressful situation less burdensome for everyone. Unfortunately, aspects of a patient's personality, appearance, or illness may sometimes appear to be the most convenient sources of this laughter. Some teams even assign humorous nicknames to their patients. Jokes about patients are inappropriate even if they remain hidden from the subjects.

4. One should consider a patient's bed to be his private property. Like the second rule, this principle mitigates a patient's feelings of lost autonomy. Such perceptions will certainly be reinforced if doctors sit on his bed without permission or put their feet on its rail while talking with him.

5. In the outpatient setting, and whenever possible in the hospital setting, one should conduct an interview while the patient is dressed, then leave the room to allow him to change into an examination gown.

6. When having an extended conversation with a patient or even a short conversation about a very important topic, one should pull up a chair and sit down. Patients appreciate this gesture because it demonstrates a commitment to the discussion and achieves a more level eye contact than is possible when the physican or student remains standing.

7. Bad news should never be communicated to a patient in the presence of the entire ward team. Instead, one or two of the team members who have been working most closely with the patient should sit down privately with him and discuss the new information.

Attire

Many clinical clerks have never before had a job that required them to dress well. Some find that they do not like the more formal clothing and prefer to wear "surgical scrubs" whenever and wherever they can. Institutions and rotations vary in the degree to which they condone this practice. Whatever the institutional policy, students must remember that one of the more difficult tasks they face is convincing their patients to treat them as doctors despite their obvious lack of experience. Regardless of what one sees on television programs, the professional image that students court is not well achieved by casual attire. Surgical scrubs should be saved for the operating room, for procedures that are likely to be particularly messy, and for sleeping when one is on call.

Family Interactions

Family members often have an extremely difficult time with their relative's illness. They may struggle without his daily presence, fear for his life, or feel guilty for not visiting more often. Some will try to make up for the patient's perceived loss of autonomy by vicariously questioning the medical team and asking them to justify their decisions. In short, families, like patients, respond to illness with a variety of attitudes and actions.

A tired and frustrated student or resident may view interactions with a patient's family as irksome and bemoan the delay they introduce in the completion of the day's work. Nevertheless, a little attention goes a long way in helping families help the patient, and *talking to the family is often the most valuable service one provides to a patient on any given day.* In addition, family members often can supply the medical team with important information that the patient is unable, or unwilling, to give.

14

A Student's Evaluations

Grades

Though clinical clerks should be most interested in learning about how to care for patients, it is perfectly understandable that they be concerned about the grades they receive on their clinical rotations, especially since these grades tend to be given great weight by review committees when students apply for residency positions at the beginning of their final year in medical school. The clerkship evaluation system may be frustrating for the students, however, because it tends to be more subjective than that used during the earlier years of medical school. Indeed, the supervising physicians' subjective impressions of a student's clinical performance form the basis for the final clerkship grade in most cases. Many rotations have written or oral examinations as well, but these are usually given less weight than the evaluations of those who have supervised the student's daily efforts on behalf of patient care.

What should the student do to ensure good clerkship evaluations? Short of writing them herself, there is nothing a student can do to *guarantee* that her evaluations will be effusively laudatory. Nevertheless, there are some key principles (Table 14-1) that will help guide any student who is eager to do well and to be rewarded

Table 14–1. The Ten Commandments of clinical clerkships

Biblical precept	Clinical precept
Thou shalt love thy neighbor as thyself.	Thou shalt know thy patients as thyself.
Thou shalt remember the Sabbath and keep it holy.	Thou shalt remember thy textbook and keep it nearby.
Thou shalt honor thy parents.	Thou shalt honor thy patients.
Thou shalt not steal.	Thou shalt not steal away to the library.
Thou shalt be fruitful and multiply.	Thy oral presentations shall be fruitful and multiple.
Thou shalt not commit adultery.	Thou shalt not commit occultery.
Thou shalt not covet thy neighbor's house.	Thou shalt not covet thy neighbor's opportunities.
Thou shalt not bear false witness against thy neighbor.	Thou shalt bear assistance to thy neighbors.
Thou shalt not kill.	Thou shalt not overkill.
Thou shalt not take the name of the Lord in vain.	Thou shalt not take thy patient's medications in vein.

for the performance. Alert readers will recognize that some of these dicta have been presented elsewhere in the text.

1. *Thou shalt know thy patients as thyself* (Chapter 9). A student must keep abreast of new symptoms, physical findings, or test results and be prepared to discuss their implications. This is not always as easy to accomplish as one might hope, because the normal routes of communication often fail to include students. Students will have to make it clear by their actions and attitudes that they want to be fully apprised of any information pertaining to their patients.

2. *Thou shalt remember thy textbook and keep it nearby* (Chapter 3). The student who researches her patients' problems with a textbook or review article will answer more questions in attending rounds, write better progress notes, give better oral presentations, and *take better care of her patients.*

3. *Thou shalt honor thy patients* (Chapters 9 and 13). An intelligent student who answers every question correctly but treats patients

poorly is unlikely to succeed. Compassion, respect, and sincere interest in one's patients are more important than obtaining the latest article from the *New England Journal of Medicine*.

4. *Thou shalt not steal away to the library* (Chapter 3). Participation in a patient's initial work-up and subsequent care is also more important than obtaining the latest article from the *New England Journal of Medicine*. Reading is of great importance, but it should not supplant patient care.

5. *Thy oral presentations shall be fruitful and multiple* (Chapter 7). Though it may not always be appropriate, a student's oral presentations have a very strong influence on the perceptions of her attendings and residents. One should therefore prepare them well and give as many as possible.

6. *Thou shalt not commit occultery* (Chapter 3). Students should not hide themselves from view. Although there is certainly no clear association between personality type and clinical competence, attendings and residents tend to give better evaluations to individuals who are extroverted and vocal and who participate actively instead of passively in clinical activities. Students who are more diffident should try at least to ask questions of their supervising physicians. A student who does not ask any questions is usually thought to be intimidated or uninterested, whereas the inquisitive student is respected for her desire to learn. Of course, one makes a better impression if the questions reflect some degree of critical analysis or prior reading.

7. *Thou shalt not covet thy neighbor's opportunities.* Attendings and residents almost always notice when a student is attempting to "show off" at the expense of one of her colleagues. One student I knew kept note cards on patients she was not following and took delight in publicly correcting her fellow students on inconsequential details about the cases. Attendings and residents realize that such unprofessional and uncharitable behavior suggests a fundamental lack of integrity and decency.

8. *Thou shalt bear assistance to thy neighbors.* Those students with a sense of "team spirit" who are willing to help other team members are likely to be appreciated and to receive better evaluations from their attendings and residents.

9. *Thou shalt not overkill.* Students should not try so hard to impress others that they appear obnoxious, insincere, or obsequious. In most cases, students will have enough opportunities to make a good impression that they need not attempt to create them.

For example, harried morning work rounds are not the appropriate setting for a student to proclaim, without apparent provocation, "I have read two recent articles on the use of immunosuppressives in inflammatory bowel disease and my interpretation is. . . ."

10. *Thou shalt not take thy patient's medications in vein.* Nursing and medical personnel prefer that all medications be taken only by the patients for whom they are prescribed. (I apologize for this pun and the attempt to end the section on a humorous note.)

Letters of Recommendation

Almost all residency programs require that two to four letters of recommendation be submitted in support of each application. Students usually obtain these letters from faculty members in the specialty they are planning to enter. It is never too early to cultivate potential sources for such letters, even if one is still undecided about a career choice. Attendings with whom one has interacted favorably may be approached as follows: "I'm not sure yet which specialty I am going to pursue, but I'd like to ask you now if you might be able to write a letter of recommendation for me in the event that I decide to go into this field." Attendings who answer affirmatively will make a mental note of the conversation. With this advance warning and a confirmation of the request as soon as the student's specialty decision has been made, they should be able to compose persuasive letters based on specific impressions rather than vague recollections.

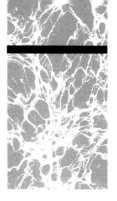

Afterword:
In Defense Of
Idealism
(with a dramatic shift to second-person
pronouns to make it more personal)

"Why do you want to go to medical school?" The question should still sound eerily familiar. Medical school admissions officers ask it with monotonous regularity—even though the most common response is somewhat predictable: "Because I want to help people." Sure, it's a bit idealistic. Sure, it's corny. Did you say it? Did you mean it?

Clerkships offer students their first real opportunity to help people, and for most medical students, this clinical work is the undisputed highlight of medical school. Lectures literally come alive on the wards, metamorphosed into patients and their clinical problems, and students finally get a chance to practice what others have preached to them in the preclinical years. They establish close and caring relationships with their patients and, in most cases, see these patients improve with therapy. With a sense of relief, they begin to comprehend more and more of the myriad interconnections among organs and diseases. They sample various specialties and get a

151

sense for which one seems most attractive. In short, students at last play the role for which so many lectures and reading assignments have been prologue.

Though the benefits are many, clinical training does have its difficulties. The care of patients, especially acutely ill inpatients, can sometimes be frustrating, discouraging, and demanding of one's time and energy. Therefore, hospital wards tend to foster a subtle cynicism among interns and residents, one in which patients are collectively viewed as "the enemy." This prevalent attitude may manifest itself in a variety of ways, from the words chosen to describe patients ("dump," "gomer," "hit," "dead liver") to the self-congratulatory celebrations that sometimes occur when a difficult patient has been transferred ("turfed" is the slang term) to another service. Those whose behavior appears to be influenced by this attitude are rarely overtly offensive or unsympathetic. They are usually good doctors and good people who are reacting in a natural way to the considerable stress imposed by their jobs. At one time or another, *all of us* lose our sense of perspective, and with it the ability to consider a patient without regard to how much work or inconvenience his care creates for us personally.

As a clinical clerk, you may eventually find yourself adopting this "us against them" mentality. Because the process can be so insidious that you don't even notice it, you may have to make a point of pausing periodically to review your actions and attitudes. If you find some that seem inconsistent with your underlying beliefs, why not attempt to recapture some of the idealism that likely imbued your response to the admissions officer? You can certainly retain a little idealism without being naive or unsophisticated. By reminding you of your actual goals, it should help make your clerkships more fun and productive. And it will undoubtedly affect your relationships with patients in ways they will appreciate.

Appendix

Common Acronyms and Abbreviations

a	Before (*ante*)
A₂	Aortic second heart sound
AAA	Abdominal aortic aneurysm
A-a gra	Alveolar to arterial oxygen tension gradient
AAL	Anterior axillary line
Ab	Antibody / Abortion
Abd	Abdomen / Abdominal
ABG	Arterial blood gas
ABI	Ankle-brachial (pressure) index
ABO	Classic blood type system
ABx	Antibiotic
ac	Before meals (*ante cibum*)
AC	Assist control (ventilator) / Air conduction
AD	Right ear (*aurio dextra*)

ADA	American Diabetes Association
ADH	Antidiuretic hormone
ad lib	As much as desired (*ad libitum*)
ADLs	Activities of daily living
AF	Afebrile/Aortofemoral
AFB	Acid-fast bacillus
Afib	Atrial fibrillation
AFL	Air-fluid level/Atrial flutter
Aflutter	Atrial flutter
AFP	Alpha-fetoprotein
AG	Antigen
AI	Aortic insufficiency
AICD	Automatic implantable cardioverter-defibrillator
AIDS	Acquired immunodeficiency syndrome
AIHA	Autoimmune hemolytic anemia
AK	Actinic keratosis
AKA	Above-the-knee amputation
AL	Left ear (*aurio laeva*)
ALL	Acute lymphocytic (lymphoblastic) leukemia
All	Allergies
ALMI	Anterolateral myocardial infarction
AMA	Against medical advice
AMI	Acute myocardial infarction
AML	Acute myelocytic leukemia
AN	Admission note
ANA	Antinuclear antibody
A&O x 3	Alert, oriented to person, place, time

AODM	Adult-onset diabetes mellitus
AP	Anteroposterior/Alkaline phosphatase
Appy	Appendectomy
ARC	AIDS-related complex
ARDS	Adult respiratory distress syndrome
ARF	Acute renal failure
AS	Aortic stenosis
ASA	Acetylsalicylic acid (aspirin)
ASAP	As soon as possible
ASCAD	Atherosclerotic coronary artery disease
ASD	Atrial septal defect
ASO	Antistreptolysin O
ASPVD	Atherosclerotic peripheral vascular disease
AST	Aspartate aminotransferase
ATNC	Atraumatic, normocephalic
AU	Both ears (*aures utrae*)
AV	Atrioventricular/Arteriovenous/Aortic valve
AVB	Atrioventricular block
AVM	Arteriovenous malformation
AVN	Atrioventricular node
AVR	Aortic valve replacement
A&W	Alive and well
AWMI	Anterior wall myocardial infarction
B	Bilateral/Both
BI/BII	Billroth's procedures

BBB	Bundle branch block
BC	Bone conduction
BCP	Birth control pills
BCx	Blood culture
BE	Barium enema/Bacterial endocarditis
bid	Twice daily (*bis in die*)
Bil dil	Biliary tract dilatation
Bili	Bilirubin level
B&J	Bone and joint
BKA	Below-the-knee amputation
BM	Bowel movement/Bone marrow
BMBx	Bone marrow biopsy
BMR	Basal metabolic rate
BMT	Bone marrow transplant
BP	Blood pressure
BPH	Benign prostatic hypertrophy
BPM	Beats per minute
BRB	Bright red blood
BRBPR	Bright red blood per rectum
BRP	Bathroom privileges
BS	Bowel sounds/Breath sounds
BSO	Bilateral salpingo-oophorectomy
BSU	Bartholin's glands, Skene's glands, and urethra
BTL	Bilateral tubal ligation
BUN	Blood urea nitrogen
BW	Body weight
Bx	Biopsy

c̄	With (*cum*)
CA	Carcinoma/Cancer
CABG	Coronary artery bypass graft operation (x 1,2,3,4 = number of grafts)
CAD	Coronary artery disease
CAH	Chronic active hepatitis
CAPD	Continuous ambulatory peritoneal dialysis
CAVH	Continuous arteriovenous hemofiltration
c/b	Complicated by
CBC	Complete blood count
CBD	Common bile duct
CBG	Capillary blood gas
CC/cc	Chief complaint/Cubic centimeter
C/C/E	Cyanosis, clubbing, edema
CCPD	Continuous cycle peritoneal dialysis
CCTV	Closed circuit television monitoring
CCU	Cardiac (intensive) care unit
CDB	Cough and deep-breathe
CEA	Carcinoembryonic antigen
CF	Cystic fibrosis
C&F	Chills and fever
CHB	Complete heart block (3° AVB)
CHD	Congenital heart disease
CHF	Congestive heart failure
CHI	Closed head injury
Choly	Cholecystectomy
CI	Cardiac index

CLL	Chronic lymphocytic leukemia
CML	Chronic myelocytic (myeloblastic) leukemia
CMT	Cervical motion tenderness
CMV	Cytomegalovirus
CN	Cranial nerve(s)
CNS	Central nervous system/Coagulase-negative staphylococcus
CO	Cardiac output
C/O	Complains of
Coags	Coagulation times
COLD	Chronic obstructive lung disease
COPD	Chronic obstructive pulmonary disease
Cor	Heart
CP	Chest pain/Cerebral palsy
CPAP	Continuous positive airway pressure
CPC	Clinicopathologic conference
CPK	Creatine phosphokinase
CPR	Cardiopulmonary resuscitation
Cr	Creatinine
CRA	Cardiorespiratory arrest
CrCl	Creatinine clearance
CRF	Chronic renal failure/Cardiac risk factors
CRI	Chronic renal insufficiency
CRP	C-reactive protein
CRT	Cadaveric renal transplant
CS	Chemstrip (blood glucose measurement)
C&S	Culture and sensitivity
CsA	Cyclosporin A

CSF	Cerebrospinal fluid
CT	Computerized tomography
CTA(P)	Clear to auscultation (and percussion)
CTSP	Called to see patient
CV	Cardiovascular / Curriculum vitae
CVA	Cerebrovascular accident / Costovertebral angle
CVP	Central venous pressure
c/w	Consistent with
CXR	Chest x-ray
d	Day/Daily
Δ	Change (Greek letter delta)
DA	Direct admission
DAW	Dispense as written
DBP	Diastolic blood pressure
D/C	Discharge/Discontinue
D&C	Dilatation and curettage
DDD	Dual-chamber paced, sensed, and triggered (pacemaker mode)
DDx	Differential diagnosis
DH	Dobhoff (feeding tube)/Dermatitis herpetiformis
DI	Diabetes insipidus
DIC	Disseminated intravascular coagulation
Dig	Digitalis
DIP	Distal interphalangeal joint
Dipy thal	Dipyridamole thallium scan
DJD	Degenerative joint disease

DKA	Diabetic ketoacidosis
DL&B	Direct laryngoscopy and biopsy
DLCO	Diffusional capacity of lungs to carbon monoxide
DM	Diabetes mellitus
DNR	Do not resuscitate
DOA	Dead on arrival
DOB	Date of birth
DOE	Dyspnea on exertion
DP	Dorsalis pedis
DPT	Diphtheria, pertussis, and tetanus
DRG	Diagnosis-related group
DTs	Delirium tremens
DTR	Deep tendon reflex
DU	Duodenal ulcer
DVT	Deep venous thrombosis
D$_5$W	5% dextrose in water
Dx	Diagnosis
dx	Disease
E→A	Egophony
EBL	Estimated blood loss
ECASA	Enteric coated aspirin
ECG	Electrocardiogram (purist's version)
Echo	Echocardiogram
ECT	Electroconvulsive therapy
EDC	Estimated date of confinement
EDTA	Ethylenediaminetetraacetic acid

EEG	Electroencephalogram
EGD	Esophagogastroduodenoscopy
EKG	Electrocardiogram (common version)
EM	Erythema multiforme
E&M	Endocrinology and metabolism
EMG	Electromyogram
EMT	Emergency medical technician
EN	Erythema nodosum
ENG	Electronystagmogram
ENT	Ear, nose, and throat
EOMI	Extraocular muscles (movement) intact
Eos	Eosinophils
EPS	Electrophysiologic study
ER	Emergency room
ERCP	Endoscopic retrograde cholangiopancreatography
ERV	Expiratory reserve volume
ESLD	End-stage liver disease
ESR	Erythrocyte sedimentation rate
ESRD	End-stage renal disease
ETOH	Alcohol (ethanol)
ETT	Exercise treadmill test/Endotracheal tube
EW	Emergency ward
Ext	Extremities
FB	Foreign body
FBS	Fasting blood sugar

F/C	Fever, chills
F/E/N	Fluids/electrolytes/nutrition
FENa	Fractional excretion of sodium
FEV$_1$	Forced expiratory volume in 1 second
FFP	Fresh frozen plasma
FH	Family history
FIO$_2$	Fraction of inspired O_2
Flex sig	Flexible sigmoidoscopy
FM	Face mask (oxygen delivery)
F→N	Finger-to-nose
FNA	Fine-needle aspiration
FOS	Full of stool
FRC	Functional residual capacity
FROM	Full range of movement
FSBG	Finger-stick blood glucose
FTA	Fluorescent treponemal antibody test
FTSG	Full-thickness skin graft
FTT	Failure to thrive
F/U	Follow-up
FUO	Fever of unknown origin
FVC	Forced vital capacity
Fx	Fracture
g	Gram
G	Gravida
GA	General anesthesia
GB	Gallbladder
GBM	Glioblastoma multiforme

GC	Gonococcus/Gonorrhea
Gent	Gentamicin
GERD	Gastroesophageal reflux disease
GES	Gastric emptying study
GFR	Glomerular filtration rate
GH	Growth hormone
GI	Gastrointestinal
GN	Glomerulonephritis
GNR	Gram-negative rods
GOO	Gastric outlet obstruction
GPC	Gram-positive cocci
GSW	Gunshot wound
GTT	Glucose tolerance test
gtt(s)	Drop(s) (*guttae*)
GU	Genitourinary
GYN	Gynecologic

HA	Headache
HAL	Hyperalimentation ("hyperal")
HAV	Hepatitis A virus
HBcAg	Hepatitis B core antigen
HBsAb	Hepatitis B surface antibody
HBsAg	Hepatitis B surface antigen
HC	Hemoccult/Hydrocortisone
HCG	Human chorionic gonadotropin
HCM	Health care maintenance
HCT	Head computerized tomogram
Hct	Hematocrit

HCTZ	Hydrochlorothiazide
HD	Hemodialysis
HDL	High-density lipoprotein
HEENT	Head, eyes, ears, nose, throat
Hgb	Hemoglobin
HgbA1c	Glycosylated hemoglobin
HH	Hiatal hernia
H/H	Hemoglobin and hematocrit
5-HIAA	5-Hydroxyindoleacetic acid
HIV	Human immunodeficiency virus
HJR	Hepatojugular reflux
HL	Heparin lock
HLA	Histocompatibility locus antigen
HME	Health maintenance examination
HMO	Health maintenance organization
HNKDC	Hyperosmolar nonketotic diabetic coma
h/o	History of
HO	House officer
HOB	Head of bed
HOH	Hard of hearing
H&P	History and physical
HPF	High-power field
HPI	History of present illness
HPV	Human papilloma virus
HR	Heart rate
hs	Bedtime (*hora somni*)
H→S	Heel to shin
HSM	Hepatosplenomegaly

HSP	Henoch-Schönlein purpura
HSV	Herpes simplex virus
HTN	Hypertension
HUS	Hemolytic-uremic syndrome
Hx	History
IAN	Intern admission note
IBD	Inflammatory bowel disease
IBS	Irritable bowel syndrome
ICM	Idiopathic cardiomyopathy
ICP	Intracranial pressure
ICS	Intercostal space
ICU	Intensive care unit
ID	Infectious disease
I&D	Incision and drainage
IDDM	Insulin-dependent diabetes mellitus
Ig	Immunoglobulin
IgEP	Immunoglobulin electrophoresis
IHD	Ischemic heart disease
IHSS	Idiopathic hypertrophic subaortic stenosis
IM	Intramuscular
IMV	Intermittent mandatory ventilation
INH	Isoniazid
I&O	Intake and output
IOP	Intraocular pressure
IP	Intraperitoneal
IPPB	Intermittent positive pressure breathing
IRDM	Insulin-requiring diabetes mellitus

ISC	Intermittent straight catheterization
IT	Intrathecal
ITP	Idiopathic thrombocytopenic purpura
IU	International unit
IUD	Intrauterine device
IV	Intravenous
IVC	Inferior vena cava
IVCD	Intraventricular conduction delay
IVDA	Intravenous drug abuse
IVF	Intravenous fluid
IVP	Intravenous pyelogram/Intravenous push
IVPB	Intravenous piggyback
IVSD	Interventricular septal defect
JAR	Junior admitting resident
JOD	Juvenile onset diabetes
JRA	Juvenile rheumatoid arthritis
JVD	Jugular venous distention
JVP	Jugular venous pressure
KF	Kayser-Fleischer
KJ	Knee jerk
KUB	Kidneys, ureters, bladder (flat/upright abdominal x-ray)
KVO	Keep vein open
L	Left/Lungs/Lobe/Lymphocyte
LA	Left atrium/Left arm

L&A   Light and accommodation

LAD   Left anterior descending coronary artery/Left axis deviation

LAE   Left atrial enlargement

LAHB   Left anterior hemiblock

LAN   Lymphadenopathy

LAP   Leukocyte alkaline phosphatase

Lat   Lateral

LBBB   Left bundle branch block

LBCD   Left border of cardiac dullness

LBP   Low back pain

LCx   Left circumflex coronary artery

LDH   Lactate dehydrogenase

LE   Lower extremity

LES   Lower esophageal sphincter

LFT   Liver function tests (bilirubin, PT/PTT, albumin)

LGV   Lymphogranuloma venereum

LH   Left heart/Luteinizing hormone/Light-headed

LIH   Left inguinal herniorrhaphy

LIT   Liver injury tests (SGOT, SGPT, LDH)

LLL   Left lower (lung) lobe

LLQ   Left lower quadrant

LMN   Lower motor neuron

LMP   Last menstrual period

LN   Lymph nodes

LOC   Loss of consciousness

LOP   Leave on pass

LP	Lumbar puncture
LPHB	Left posterior hemiblock
LPN	Licensed practical nurse
LRD	Living related donor
LS	Lumbo-sacral
LSB	Left sternal border
LUL	Left upper (lung) lobe
LUQ	Left upper quadrant
LV	Left ventricle
LVEDP	Left ventricular end-diastolic pressure
LVH	Left ventricular hypertrophy
MAL	Midaxillary line
MAP	Mean arterial pressure
MAT	Multifocal atrial tachycardia
MB	Myocardial CPK band
MCA	Middle cerebral artery
MCH	Mean corpuscular hemoglobin
MCHC	Mean corpuscular hemoglobin concentration
MCL	Midclavicular line
MCP	Metacarpal-phalangeal joint
MCV	Mean corpuscular volume
MDI	Metered-dose inhaler
Med	Medication
MEN	Multiple endocrine neoplasia
MI	Myocardial infarction
MLE	Midline episiotomy
MM	Multiple myeloma

MMR	Measles, mumps, rubella
MOM	Milk of magnesia
Mono	Mononucleosis
MR	Mitral regurgitation/Mental retardation
m,r,g	Murmurs, rubs, gallops
MRI	Magnetic resonance imaging
MRSA	Methicillin-resistant *Staphylococcus aureus*
MRSE	Methicillin-resistant *Staphylococcus epidermidis*
MS	Mental status/Mitral stenosis/Multiple sclerosis/Morphine sulfate
MSSA	Methicillin-sensitive *Staphylococcus aureus*
MSSE	Methicillin-sensitive *Staphylococcus epidermidis*
MTP	Metatarsal-phalangeal joint
MUGA	MUltiGAted nuclear ventriculogram
MV	Mitral valve
MVA	Motor vehicle accident
MVR	Mitral valve replacement
NA	Not applicable
NABS	Normoactive bowel sounds
NAD	No active disease/No acute distress
NAS	No added salt
NC	Nasal cannula (oxygen delivery)/No change
NCAT	Normocephalic, atraumatic
NCV	Nerve conduction velocity
NED	No evidence of disease
NG	Nasogastric
NH	Nursing home

NHL	Non-Hodgkin's lymphoma
NIDDM	Non–insulin-dependent diabetes mellitus
NKA	No known allergies
NKDA	No known drug allergies
NL	Normal
NMT	Nebulized mist treatment
NOC	Night (nocturnal)
NPH	Neutral-protamine-Hagedorn (intermediate-acting insulin)
NPO	Nothing by mouth (*nil per os*)
NPV	Negative predictive value
NR	Nonreactive
NS	Normal saline
NSAID	Nonsteroidal anti-inflammatory drug
NSR	Normal sinus rhythm
NSST	Nonspecific ST segment changes
NSVT	Nonsustained ventricular tachycardia
NTG	Nitroglycerin
NTND	Nontender, nondistended
N/V	Nausea, vomiting
NVD	Nausea, vomiting, diarrhea
O_2	Oxygen
OA	Osteoarthritis
OB	Obstetrics
OBS	Organic brain syndrome
OCG	Oral cholecystogram
OD	Right eye (*oculus dextro*)/Overdose

OLT	Orthotopic liver transplant
OM	Obtuse marginal coronary artery/Otitis media
OOB	Out of bed
OP	Oropharynx
O&P	Ova and parasites
OR	Operating room
ORIF	Open reduction, internal fixation
OS	Left eye (*oculus sinistro*)/Opening snap
OSH	Outside hospital
OT	Occupational therapy
OU	Both eyes (*oculo utro*)
o/w	Otherwise
P	Para/Pulse
p̄	Post (after)
P$_2$	Pulmonic second heart sound
PA	Posterior-anterior/Physician's assistant/Pulmonary artery
P&A	Percussion and auscultation
PAC	Premature atrial contraction
PAF	Paroxysmal atrial fibrillation
PAN	Polyarteritis nodosa
PAO$_2$	Alveolar oxygen pressure
PaO$_2$	Arterial partial pressure of oxygen
PAP	Pulmonary artery pressure
PAS	Para-aminosalicylic acid
PAT	Paroxysmal atrial tachycardia

PAWP	Pulmonary artery wedge pressure
PBC	Primary biliary cirrhosis
pc	After meals (*post cibum*)
PCA	Patient-controlled analgesia pump
PCKD	Polycystic kidney disease
PCN	Penicillin
PCOD	Polycystic ovary disease
PCP	*Pneumocystis carinii* pneumonia/Phencyclidine
PCWP	Pulmonary capillary wedge pressure
PDA	Patent ductus arteriosus
PDR	*Physicians' Desk Reference*
PE	Pulmonary embolism/Physical examination
PEEP	Positive end-expiratory pressure
PEG	Percutaneous gastric (tube)/Polyethylene glycol
PERRL(A)	Pupils equally round and reactive to light (and accommodation)
PET	Positron emission tomography
PFT	Pulmonary function testing
PI	Pulmonic insufficiency/Principal investigator
PID	Pelvic inflammatory disease
PIP	Proximal interphalangeal joint
PJC	Premature junctional complex
PKU	Phenylketonuria
Plts	Platelets
PMH	Past medical history
PMI	Point of maximum impulse

PMN	Polymorphonuclear leukocyte
PMR	Polymyalgia rheumatica
PM&R	Physical medicine and rehabilitation
PMS	Premenstrual syndrome
PN	Progress note
PND	Paroxysmal nocturnal dyspnea
PNH	Paroxysmal nocturnal hemoglobinuria
PO	By mouth (*per os*)
POD	Postoperative day
PPD	Purified protein derivative (TB skin test)
P&PD	Percussion and postural drainage
PPO	Preferred provider organization
PPV	Positive predictive value
PR	Per rectum
prn	When necessary (*pro re nata*)
PS	Pulmonic stenosis
PSA	Prostate-specific antigen
PSH	Past surgical history
PSS	Progressive systemic sclerosis
PSVT	Paroxysmal supraventricular tachycardia
Pt	Patient
PT	Prothrombin time / Physical therapy
PTA	Prior to admission
PTCA	Percutaneous transluminal coronary angioplasty
PTH	Parathyroid hormone
PTT	Partial thromboplastin time
PUD	Peptic ulcer disease

PUVA Psoralen, ultraviolet A treatment (for psoriasis)

PV Pulmonic valve

P&V Pyloroplasty and vagotomy

PVC Premature ventricular contraction

PVOD Peripheral vascular occlusive disease

PVR Postvoid residual

q Each, every (*quaque*)

Q Perfusion

qd Each day

qhs Every night before sleep

qid Four times a day (*quarter in die*)

QNS Quantity not sufficient

qod Every other day

R Respirations

RA Rheumatoid arthritis/Right atrium/Room air

RAD Right axis deviation

RAN Resident admission note

RAP Right atrial pressure

RBBB Right bundle branch block

RBC Red blood cell

RCA Right coronary artery

RDW Red cell distribution width

RFA Radiofrequency ablation

RHD Rheumatic heart disease

RIA	Radioimmunoassay
RIND	Reversible ischemic neurologic deficit
RLL	Right lower (lung) lobe
RLQ	Right lower quadrant
RML	Right middle (lung) lobe
RN	Registered nurse
RND	Radical neck dissection
R/O	Rule out
ROM	Range of motion
ROS	Review of systems
RPGN	Rapidly progressive glomerulonephritis
RPR	Rapid plasma reagin test (syphilis)
RR	Respiratory rate
RRA	Radioreceptor assay (serum pregnancy test)
RRR	Regular rate and rhythm
RSB	Right sternal border
RT	Respiratory therapy/Radiation therapy
RTA	Renal tubular acidosis
RTC	Return to clinic
RUL	Right upper (lung) lobe
RUQ	Right upper quadrant
RV	Residual volume/Right ventricle
RVH	Right ventricular hypertrophy
Rx	Prescription/Therapy/Treatment
$\overline{s}$	Without (*sans*)
S_1	First heart sound
S_2	Second heart sound

S_3	Third heart sound
S_4	Fourth heart sound
SA	Sinoatrial
SAH	Subarachnoid hemorrhage
SAN	Sinoatrial node
SAR	Senior admitting resident
SBE	Subacute bacterial endocarditis
SBFT	Small bowel follow-through
SBO	Small bowel obstruction
SC	Subcutaneously
SCA	Sickle cell anemia
SCCA	Squamous cell carcinoma
SCID	Severe combined immunodeficiency
SCM	Sternocleidomastoid
SEM	Systolic ejection murmur
SG	Swan-Ganz
SGA	Small for gestational age
SH	Social history
SI	Sacroiliac
SIADH	Syndrome of inappropriate antidiuretic hormone
SICU	Surgical intensive care unit
Sig	To be written (*signa* = "mark thou")
SK	Seborrheic keratosis
SL	Sublingually
SLE	Systemic lupus erythematosus
SOB	Short(ness) of breath
s/p	Status post (now after)

SPEP	Serum protein electrophoresis
SQ	Subcutaneously
S/S	Signs, symptoms
SSCP	Substernal chest pain
SSS	Sick sinus syndrome
Stat	Immediately (*statim*)
STD	Sexually transmitted disease
Stress thal	Stress (exercise) thallium test
SVC	Superior vena cava
SVG	Spontaneous vaginal delivery
SVT	Sustained ventricular tachycardia/Supraventricular tachycardia
Sx	Symptoms
sx	Surgery
T	Temperature
T$_3$	Triiodothyronine
T$_4$	Tetraiodothyronine
T&A	Tonsillectomy and adenoidectomy
TAH	Total abdominal hysterectomy
TB	Tuberculosis
TBA	To be announced
TBG	Thyroid-binding globulin
TBI	Traumatic brain injury
T&C	Type and cross of blood
TCT	Thrombin clotting time
TEE	Transesophageal echocardiogram
TFTs	Thyroid function tests

TI	Tricuspid insufficiency
TIA	Transient ischemic attack
TIBC	Total iron-binding capacity
TICU	Thoracic intensive care unit/Transplant intensive care unit/Trauma intensive care unit
TID	Three times a day (*ter in die*)
TKO	To keep open
TLC	Total lung capacity/Tender loving care
TM	Tympanic membrane
TMC	Triamcinolone
TMJ	Temporomandibular joint
TMP/SMX	Trimethoprim-sulfamethoxazole
TNTC	Too numerous to count
TO	Telephone order
TP	Total protein
tPA	Tissue plasminogen activator
TPN	Total parenteral nutrition
TPR	Temperature, pulse, respirations
tra	To run at (IV fluid rate)
TS	Tricuspid stenosis
T&S	Type and screen
TSH	Thyroid-stimulating hormone
TTP	Thrombotic thrombocytopenic purpura
TTT	Tilt table test
TURP	Transurethral resection of prostate
TV	Total volume/Tidal volume
TWI	T-wave inversion

Tx	Treatment
tx	Tissue
txp	Transplant
U	Unit
UA	Urinalysis
UC	Ulcerative colitis
UE	Upper extremity
UGI	Upper gastrointestinal
UGIB	Upper gastrointestinal bleed(ing)
UMN	Upper motor neuron
UQ	Upper quadrant
URI	Upper respiratory infection
US	Ultrasound
USA	Unstable angina
USOH	Usual state of health
UTI	Urinary tract infection
UV	Ultraviolet
VA	Veterans Administration
VC	Vital capacity
VCUG	Voiding cystourethrogram
VD	Venereal disease
VDRL	Venereal Disease Research Laboratory (syphilis test)
Vfib (VF)	Ventricular fibrillation
VMA	Vanillylmandelic acid
VO	Verbal or voice order

VP	Ventriculoperitoneal
V̇/Q̇	Ventilation-perfusion
VS	Vital signs
VSD	Ventricular septal defect
VSS	Vital signs stable
Vtach (VT)	Ventricular tachycardia
VV	Veins
VVI	Ventricular paced, sensed, and inhibited (pacemaker mode)
VVV	Ventricular paced, sensed, and triggered (pacemaker mode)
VWF	von Willebrand's factor
WBC	White blood count/White blood cells
W/D	Withdrawal
WN	Well-nourished
WNL	Within normal limits
w/o	Without
WPW	Wolff-Parkinson-White syndrome
w/u	Work-up
x̄	Except
XRT	X-ray therapy
yo	Years old
ZES	Zollinger-Ellison syndrome

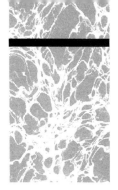

Index

Telephone Numbers

Notes

Notes

Notes

Instructions for the Use of Detachable Pages

Outline of History and Physical Examination

The page should be detached and folded in half along the guide to create a small booklet that can easily fit into a shirt or lab coat pocket. The front page of the booklet is an outline of the components of the interview. Students should remember that the structure is somewhat arbitrary and is really more important to the presentation than to the interview. A good interviewer will often follow the patient from one topic to another in order to avoid discontinuity and awkwardness. (See Chapter 4 for further details.) The center pages list symptoms commonly elicited in the review of systems. For convenience, some clinicians reserve certain questions from the other parts of the history for inclusion here. These have been placed in parentheses. The back page offers one approach to the "complete" physical examination. It is presented in categorical outline, without great detail, so that it may better serve as an "at a glance" reminder to students without being obvious to the patients they are examining. As with the history format, the order is clearly arbitrary and better represents a standard presentation sequence than the examination process itself. Other approaches, as long as they are used consistently, can work just as well.

Patient Data Note Card

This page represents a miniaturized version of the patient data card discussed in Chapter 10. To be used in the manner described, it must be enlarged to 5 1/2 x 8 1/2 inches:

    1. Detach the page and take it to a local copy center. (Show them these instructions, if you like, and ask for their assistance in performing the steps properly.)

    2. Ask them to copy each side twice onto 8 1/2 x 11 paper at a magnification of exactly 137 percent. Take your copy of the book with you and show them this page so that they know the author and publisher grant permission for the duplication and do not consider it copyright infringement.

    3. Using a paper cutter or an X-acto knife, carefully cut around the perimeter of each of the four rectangles, just inside the lines, to create four paper note cards that are approximately 5 1/2 x 8 1/2 and have no bordering lines.

    4. Take an 8 1/2 x 11 sheet of blank paper and loosely paste the four enlarged note cards onto it in such a way that the two card fronts are side by side on one side and the two card backs are adjacent on the other. Because the four rectangles will be slightly smaller than 5 1/2 x 8 1/2, it is important that they be placed properly on the larger sheet of paper; the outer, top corner of each rectangle should be aligned exactly with the corresponding corner of the 8 1/2 x 11 sheet of blank paper. Make a test copy to be sure no text is being cut off on the edges.

    5. Ask that this piece of paper, both front and back, be copied onto card stock paper (white works best, though other colors may be used) and then cut down the center so that two cards are created from each copy. Have them make as many as you wish.

    6. If the cards prove useful, keep the 8 1/2 x 11 sheet from step four to use as a template for future reproductions.